LOWER NEW ENGLAND

The Jared Coffin House, Nantucket

COUNTRY INNS OF AMERICA

Lower New England

A GUIDE TO THE INNS OF
MASSACHUSETTS, CONNECTICUT, AND RHODE ISLAND

BY ROBERTA HOMAN GARDNER
WITH
TERRY BERGER, GEORGE ALLEN, AND TRACY ECCLESINE

PHOTOGRAPHS BY GEORGE W. GARDNER AND LILO RAYMOND
DESIGNED AND PRODUCED BY ROBERT REID AND TERRY BERGER

HOLT, RINEHART AND WINSTON, *New York*

Cover: The Victorian, Whitinsville, Massachusetts.

Frontispiece: The Inn at Castle Hill, Newport, Rhode Island.

Maps, Anthony St. Aubyn.
Editorial assistance, Christine Timmons.

Photographs on the following pages are used with permission from The Knapp Press, 5900 Wilshire Blvd, Los Angeles, CA 90036, © 1978 and 1980 by Knapp Communications Corporation: 1, 8–11, 18–21, 32, 33, 35, 40, 41, 43–45, 56–60, 62–63, 72, 73, 77–87, 94–99, 101, 104–105, 108, 110.

Photographs on the following pages are used with permission: 34; 111, 112 (photographs by Jim Raycroft).

Library of Congress Cataloging in Publication Data

Gardner, Roberta Homan.
    Lower New England, a guide to the inns of Massachusetts, Connecticut, and Rhode Island.

    (Country inns of America)
    Rev. ed. of: Lower New England, a guide to the inns of Connecticut, Massachusetts, and Rhode Island / by Peter Andrews, George Allen, and Tracy Ecclesine. 1st ed. 1980.
    1. Hotels, taverns, etc.—Connecticut—Directories.
2. Hotels, taverns, etc.—Massachusetts—Directories.
3. Hotels, taverns, etc.—Rhode Island—Directories.
1. Andrews, Peter, 1931–   . Lower New England, a guide to the inns of Connecticut, Massachusetts, and Rhode Island.   II. Title.   III. Series.
TX907.A6625   1985   647′.947401   85–883
ISBN 0–03–003319–5

First Edition

10 9 8 7 6 5 4 3 2 1

A Robert Reid / Terry Berger production
Typeset in Sabon Roman by Monotype Composition Company, Inc., Baltimore, Maryland.
Printed and bound by Mandarin Offset International, Ltd., Hong Kong

ISBN 0-03-003319-5

THE INNS

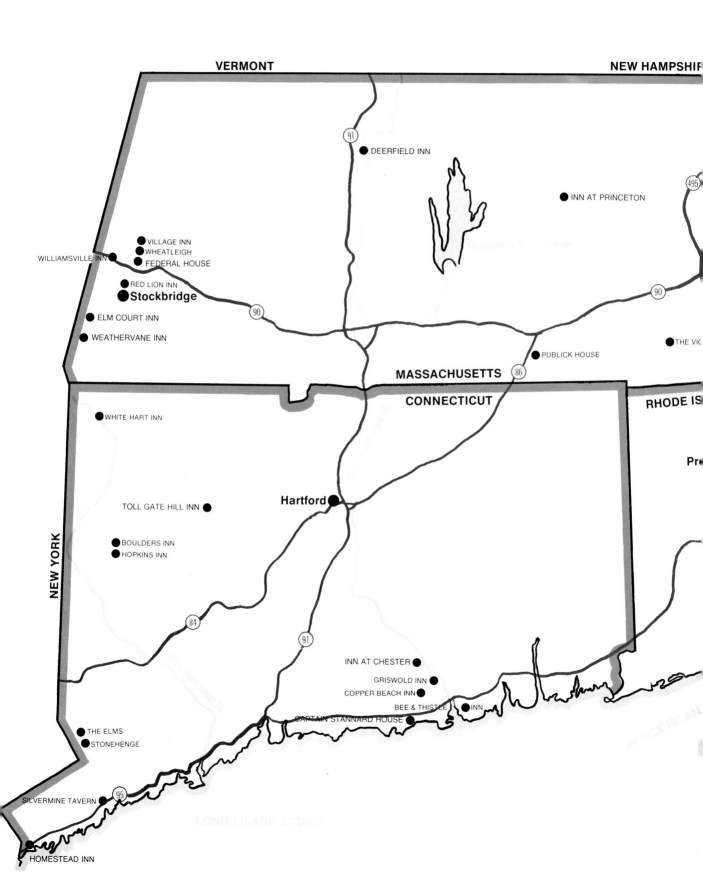

VERMONT

NEW HAMPSHIRE

91

● DEERFIELD INN

495

● INN AT PRINCETON

● VILLAGE INN
● WHEATLEIGH
● FEDERAL HOUSE

WILLIAMSVILLE INN ●

90

● RED LION INN

● **Stockbridge**

● ELM COURT INN

90

● WEATHERVANE INN

MASSACHUSETTS

● THE VIC

● PUBLICK HOUSE

86

CONNECTICUT

RHODE IS

● WHITE HART INN

Pr

NEW YORK

TOLL GATE HILL INN ●

Hartford ●

● BOULDERS INN
● HOPKINS INN

84

91

INN AT CHESTER ●

GRISWOLD INN ●

COPPER BEACH INN ●

BEE & THISTLE ● INN

● THE ELMS

CAPTAIN STANNARD HOUSE ●

● STONEHENGE

95

SILVERMINE TAVERN ●

LONG ISLAND SOUND

BLACK ISLAND

HOMESTEAD INN

EDITOR'S NOTE

Country inns have come a long way since the first edition of this book was published. New England has always abounded in inns, but the high standards of sophistication that now prevail, in both food and décor, make it possible to produce a new, upscaled inn guide that will appeal to the most experienced inn-goer as well as attract new travelers to the wonderful world of country inns.

There is still a good variety of inns represented. Some are notable for their food, others for their restoration and furnishings, and still others for their historical and architectural interest. Some, of course, are worth visiting because of their special innkeepers.

Rather than give specific rates, as they are always subject to change, we have designated rates as *inexpensive, moderate,* or *expensive*. This means that we consider

under $45 per double room *inexpensive;*
$45 to $85 per double room *moderate;* and
over $85 per double room *expensive.*

Since many inns now charge per room, rather than for singles or doubles, it would behoove single occupants to check rates carefully.

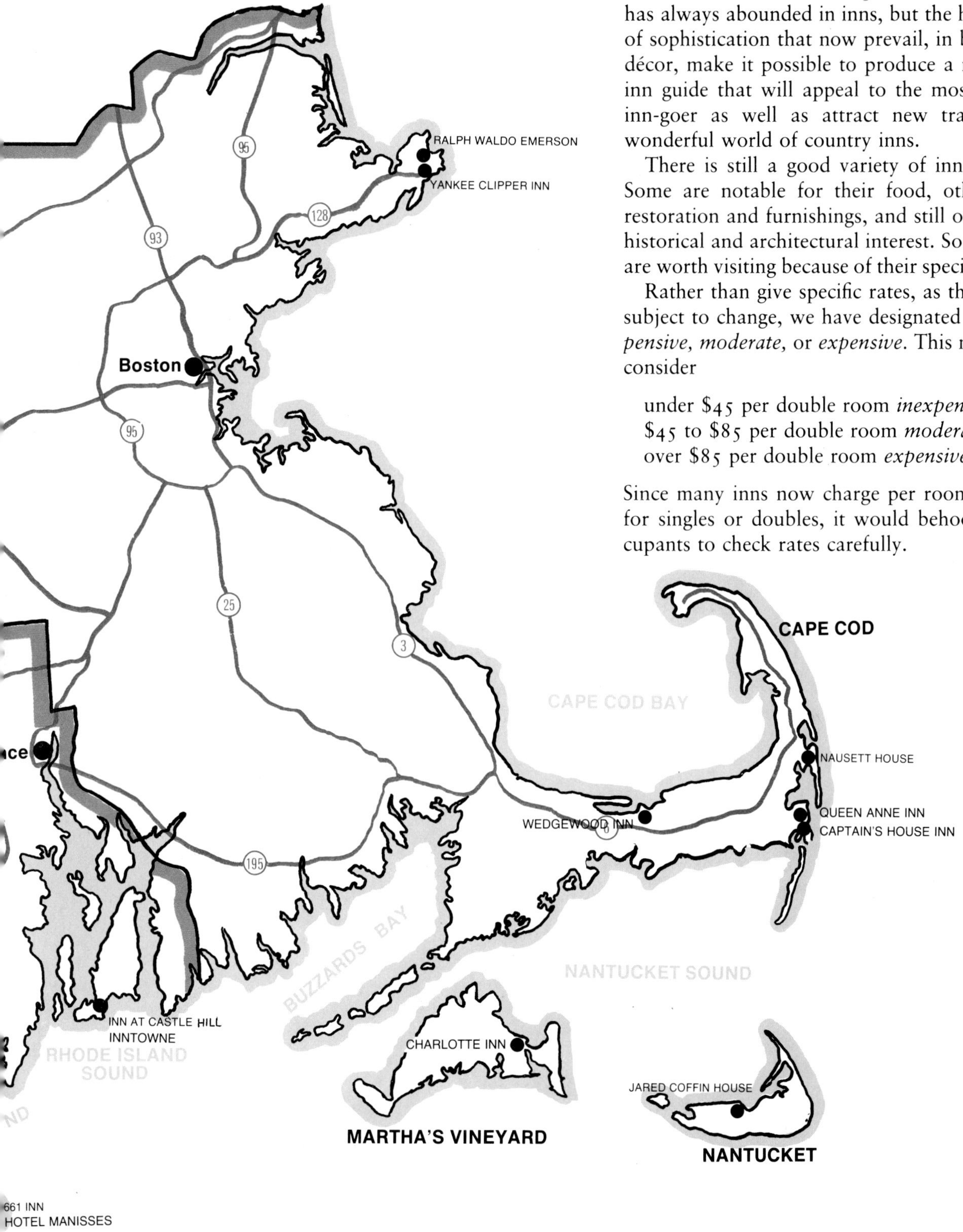

RALPH WALDO EMERSON

YANKEE CLIPPER INN

Boston

CAPE COD

CAPE COD BAY

NAUSETT HOUSE

WEDGEWOOD INN

QUEEN ANNE INN
CAPTAIN'S HOUSE INN

NANTUCKET SOUND

BUZZARDS BAY

INN AT CASTLE HILL
INNTOWNE

RHODE ISLAND SOUND

CHARLOTTE INN

JARED COFFIN HOUSE

MARTHA'S VINEYARD

NANTUCKET

661 INN
HOTEL MANISSES

MASSACHUSETTS

One of the great New England inns

Set twenty-five miles south of Cape Cod in the Atlantic Ocean, Nantucket Island offers visitors a dramatic change of pace and ready entry into the rich history of New England. Discovered in 1602, the island served as a major whaling port in the eighteenth and nineteenth centuries, and today awareness of that past is kept palpably alive both by the island's brick sidewalks and cobblestone streets and by the marvelous collections in the local Folger Museum and The Whaling Museum.

Among those involved in the island's nineteenth-century trade was wealthy shipowner Jared Coffin, who in 1845 proclaimed his good fortune by building the largest mansion on the island.

Over the years Coffin's house changed hands a number of times, with each owner making additions and changes to the structure—not all of them propitious. In 1961 The Nantucket Historical Trust purchased the home and painstakingly restored it as part of the restoration plan for the whole island. In turn, Philip and Peggy Read bought the Greek Revival structure and with considerable care and work transformed it into one of the finest inns in New England.

Filled with period antiques and oriental rugs, the original Jared Coffin House is actually one of six buildings that comprise the inn. Most of the other buildings are also nineteenth-century structures and are furnished with period reproductions, offering, like the Jared Coffin House itself, spacious guest rooms with canopy four-poster beds. Only the Daniel Webster House, built in 1964, is furnished with contemporary furniture, and this building is scheduled to soon undergo major renovation to "gently age" its décor and make it compatible with the rest of the inn.

Daniel Webster House, all with private baths, some with showers only. Two restaurants, both open to the public: The Taproom serves lunch and dinner year round; JARED's serves breakfast and dinner daily May through October, on weekends and holidays in November, December, and March, and is closed January through March. Children welcome, with advance arrangements; well-behaved pets welcome; all major credit cards accepted. Confirmed reservations imperative.

DIRECTIONS: Woods Hole, Mass., ferry runs mid-June to mid-September and January through March. Hyannis, Mass., ferry runs April through December. For information and mandatory advance automobile reservations, call (617) 540-2022. Air service is available year round from Boston, New York, and Hyannis.

JARED COFFIN HOUSE, 29 Broad St., Nantucket Island, MA 02554; (617) 228-2400; Philip and Margaret Read, Innkeepers. Rates: *moderate* to *expensive*. Open year round; 9 rooms in Jared Coffin House, 16 in 1857 Eben Allen wing, 3 in 18th-century Swain House, 6 in 1821 Henry Coffin House, 12 in 1842 Harrison Gray House, 12 in

PREVIOUS PAGE: Nantucket harbor wharf, lined with private houses. *Left:* Guest rooms in the fully restored 1845 mansion.

A truly special inn on Martha's Vineyard

Wandering down a sun-dappled side street close to the Edgartown harbor, one comes upon a clutch of beautifully tended buildings, each with a character and style all its own. You've arrived at the Charlotte Inn. Innkeepers Paula and Gery Conover know instinctively what makes an inn great, and they strive to see that the Charlotte ranks among America's best.

Guests enter the Main House, shaded by a towering chestnut tree, to check in at the gleaming antique English barrister's desk tucked away behind the staircase. Your own private haven may be waiting in this 1860s-vintage sea captain's home, lovely with its arched shutters and graceful widow's walk; in the Carriage House, a private bower nestled in an English

Left: Chez Pierre, the inn's restaurant, is noted for its romantic setting and impeccable food.

garden; in the colonial Garden House across the street; or in the newly renovated Summer House next door.

The Main House's immaculate bedrooms are furnished in traditional American and English antiques—sleigh beds and four-posters, tufted chaises and wicker rockers, exquisitely upholstered wingback and over-stuffed reading chairs. The Carriage House, reminiscent of an English country cottage, contains two bedrooms at garden level and a second-story suite. In this luxurious hideaway, matching French doors flank the entire chamber and look out over quaint latticework fences, landscaped gardens, and a private patio. In keeping with its more casual demeanor, the Garden House is decorated in "American country" with fine print fabrics, colorful quilts, iron and brass and other antique bedsteads, while the Summer House, with its broad veranda filled with wicker furniture, is like an old-fashioned romantic valentine. No matter where guests rest their heads, they will savor the elegance and softness of this most special inn.

The first floor of the main inn is an art gallery featuring American and English painters, who excel

A marble fireplace graces a guest room in the Main House.

in lyrical landscapes and seascapes, and this floor also houses a small shop carrying a grand array of fine decorative objects. Just behind the gallery is Chez Pierre, a romantic garden restaurant, where gifted chef Eniko DeLisle creates her special cuisine. Eniko seeks out the freshest foodstuffs available, flying in produce from as far away as Europe, and she has gained a reputation for sublime food beautifully served by a congenial and knowledgeable staff.

CHARLOTTE INN, 27 S. Summer St., Edgartown, MA 02539; (617) 627-4751; Paula and Gery Conover, and Gery, Jr., and Timmy Conover, Innkeepers. Rates: *moderate* to *expensive;* continental breakfast included. Open year round; 24 rooms in inn, all with private baths. Dining room serves dinner nightly in summer; in off-season, serves dinner and Sunday brunch on weekends. No children; no pets; Visa, MasterCard accepted. The hamlet of Edgartown has a protected harbor and is filled with fine shops; the island itself offers wonderful beaches and good restaurants.

DIRECTIONS: Take the ferry from Wood's Hole, Mass., to Vineyard Haven. From the ferry, follow signs to Edgartown, where you should turn right off Main St. onto S. Summer St. Inn is ½ block on left. *Note:* Ferry reservations are mandatory for passengers with cars and should be made well in advance.

The Main House. OVERLEAF: Guests check in at this gleaming antique barrister's desk.

Guest rooms in the Main House are consistently fresh and elegant, *above* and *right*.

| East Orleans | NAUSET HOUSE | MASSACHUSETTS |

Where physical beauty and fine spirits co-exist

The warmth and generosity of innkeepers Diane and Al Johnson spill over and pervade the Nauset House. To ensure that each guest thoroughly enjoys Cape Cod, the Johnsons go out of their way to guide newcomers to a host of wonderful discoveries and experiences.

In honor of the natural beauty indigenous to the area, each bedroom is named after a type of Cape flora—Beach Plum, Mayflower, Sea Oats, Wild Strawberries, to name a few. Colorful stencils, whimsical hand-painted renderings, or everlasting bouquets of grasses related to each namesake, appear in all of the rooms.

Diane, an accomplished artist, constantly adds thoughtful and lovely touches to all the guest rooms. Her leaded glass lamps, windows, and picture frames grace many tables and walls throughout the inn. She also collects and displays the work of gifted artisans, such as Nancy Craemer, whose fanciful ceramic birdbath, complete with miniature bathing hippos, is tucked into the lush foliage of the inn's greenhouse conservatory.

This is one of the Nauset's special hideaways, a crystal pavilion with bricked floor, white wicker furniture, and a forest of plants and trees. The greenhouse adjoins the inn's dining room, whose stucco walls, dark beams, open hearth, and copper bar create a rustic, yet sophisticated atmosphere. The dining room also has a wall of glass, which opens onto a brick patio shaded by handsome, old apple trees. Guest rooms are located in the shingle-and-clapboard main house, in the Carriage House, and in a shed-like retreat called "the outermost house." The latter, which was at one time a feed storage barn, can accommodate one couple. It is a charming and simple dollhouse with rough-hewn floor and ceiling boards, a bed built into the old feed bin, a sliding glass door, and a large bathroom window that looks out onto a private fenced yard. The remainder of the bedchambers in the inn are furnished with antiques—ornate Victorian, simple iron and

Left: The breakfast room is filled with authentic Early American pieces. OVERLEAF: The fine old clapboard inn building is as New England as you can get.

The sitting room.

brass, and sturdy four-poster beds, a variety of old-fashioned chairs and sofas, hooked and rag rugs—accompanied by an array of traditional pieces.

The Nauset House is one of those rare and fortunate inns whose physical beauties, which exist in abundance, are outweighed only by the fine spirit of its innkeepers.

NAUSET HOUSE INN, P.O. Box 446, Beach Rd., East Orleans, MA 02643; (617) 225-2195; Diane and Al Johnson, Owners, John Vessela, Manager. Rates: *moderate.* Open first weekend in April through last weekend in October; 9 rooms in inn, 4 in Carriage House, 1 in "outermost house," with private and shared baths, some with showers only. Dining room, open to inn guests only, serves breakfast daily. No bar; guests may bring liquor. No children under 12; no pets; Visa, MasterCard accepted. Tennis, golf, riding, swimming, sailing nearby.

DIRECTIONS: From Rte. 6 on Cape Cod, take exit 12 and follow small signs to Nauset Beach. Inn is on Nauset Beach Rd., ½ mile before the beach.

QUEEN ANNE INN

An intimate getaway on Cape Cod

Of all the small communities that dot the Cape Cod peninsula, Chatham is among the most successful at maintaining its heritage as a sea-going village rather than a tourist encampment. The Queen Anne, a rambling, grey-shingled inn located in the central section of Chatham, offers travelers an opportunity to discover the beauties of this village. Innkeeper Guenther Weinkopf is a veteran hotelier, who takes pride in running his inn like a quality hotel, all the while retaining the warm ambience of an intimate getaway.

His ambition fully succeeds, most especially in the food department. The Earl of Chatham restaurant is renowned for its thoughtfully prepared and beautifully presented cuisine. The dining room is a lovely reflection of Guenther's Austrian heritage, with its gleaming hardwood floor, dove grey walls, dusty rose and richly patterned draperies, and a plate rail neatly lined with crockery and beer steins. The menu changes with the seasons; just to read a selection of entrées sets one's mouth watering. Consider starting a meal with succulent dumplings dressed with bacon, goat cheese, and sour cream; a delicate homemade sausage—a mélange of sweetbreads and veal with wild mushrooms and truffles in a green peppercorn sauce; or warm discs of goat cheese layered on watercress and Belgian endive and napped with a creamy mustard dressing. The chef takes full advantage of his proximity to the sea with such main course offerings as fresh Atlantic salmon with a salmon mousse steamed in Boston lettuce, and dressed with chive beurre blanc, or paupiettes of grey sole with spinach mousse and fresh crabmeat in a champagne sauce. Desserts, all made fresh in the kitchen, are equally delectable and irresistable.

In 1840 the Queen Anne was built as a private home; it opened as an inn at the turn of the century. To accommodate the ever-burgeoning flow of guests, two wings were added in the middle of this century. The inn's backyard, whose centerpiece is the chef's

Left: A colorful fixture in the inn's back yard is the chef's herb garden. OVERLEAF: The entryway, *left,* opens onto two sitting rooms, one of which, *right,* is a pre-dinner gathering spot.

The inn's dining room.

flourishing herb garden, faces out toward the tranquil Oyster Pond Bay. Rooms on this side of the inn are blessed with large patios that take full advantage of the view. All of the guest rooms are furnished with an eclectic mix of antiques, and each is spotlessly maintained.

QUEEN ANNE INN, 70 Queen Anne Rd., Chatham, MA 02633; (617) 945-0394; Guenther Weinkopf, Innkeeper. Rates: *moderate* to *expensive*; continental breakfast included. Open Easter through Thanksgiving; 28 rooms in inn, 2 in cottage, all with private baths. Restaurant, open to the public, serves breakfast and dinner daily. Children welcome; no pets; Visa, MasterCard accepted. Clay tennis courts on premises as well as a power boat for excursions; beach, antiquing nearby.

DIRECTIONS: Take Rte. 6 (Mid-Cape Hwy.) to exit 11. Drive south on Rte. 137 until it ends, joining with Rte. 28. Turn left on Rte. 28 and at the first traffic light (about 3 miles), bear right onto Queen Anne Rd. Inn is immediately on the right.

CAPTAIN'S HOUSE INN

Chatham   MASSACHUSETTS

Nurturing hosts at an impressive inn

A magnificent, immaculately trimmed, eight-foot privet hedge secludes the Captain's House from the rest of the world. This impressive wall of greenery is so handsome it compels one to explore further. What visitors soon discover is an inn as immaculate and impressive as the carefully tended hedge.

The Captain's House is a Greek Revival sea captain's home, white clapboard with black shutters, that was built by prosperous packet skipper Hiram Harding in the mid-1800s. The entryway and adjoining formal parlor are furnished with a fine selection of Chippendale and Queen Anne chairs and tables, styles that perfectly complement the classic lines of

Left: A glimpse of the Eliza Jane Room, with its antique bird's-eye maple canopy bed, seen from the Williamsburg-style living room.

the house. Each antique-filled guest room is named after a ship that Captain Harding sailed. The Hannah Rebekah is captivating with its antique four-poster canopy bed, dressed in luxurious white-ruffled linens. Fresh floral wallpaper, a celery green loveseat, a handsome hardwood floor warmed by handhooked rugs, a wing chair and hassock covered in rich crewel upholstery, and a working fireplace at the foot of the bed set a mood of intimacy and romance. The remainder of the rooms in the house, from the Eliza Jane with its magnificent antique bird's-eye maple canopy bed to sweet and old-fashioned Clarissa, are consistently charming and comfortable.

The Captain's Cottage, a grey shingled, bow-roofed, Cape Cod cottage, is located a few yards away from the inn proper, and it contains two especially beautiful bedrooms. The interior of the cottage is from a two-centuries-old New England home, and innkeepers Cathy and Dave Eakin have carefully preserved its rich colonial character.

Every morning Cathy and Dave wake early to prepare for breakfast. Dave sets out for the morning newspaper while Cathy whips up a variety of homemade sweet breads, coffeecakes, or muffins. Soon the

first early risers wander into the sunporch breakfast room, just off the parlor. Many guests enjoy perusing the paper, catching up with the day's news. Others are content to sip their coffee and let the world go by. The Captain's House is a perfect place to escape from the world.

CAPTAIN'S HOUSE INN, 371 Old Harbor Rd., Chatham, MA 02633; (617) 945-0217; Cathy and Dave Eakin, Innkeepers. Rates; *moderate* to *expensive;* continental breakfast included. Open year round, except from after New Year's weekend to Washington's Birthday (3rd weekend in February); advance reservations mandatory; 11 rooms in inn, one 3-bedroom carriage house, all with private bath, some with shower only. No dining room; no bar, though guests may bring liquor. Children under 12 welcome in Carriage House only; no pets; Visa, MasterCard, American Express accepted. Golf, tennis, shopping, beach, sightseeing nearby.

DIRECTIONS: From New York City or Boston, cross the Cape Cod Canal at the Sagamore Bridge and follow the Mid-Cape Hwy. (Rte. 6) to exit 11 (Rte. 137) and Rte. 137 south to Rte. 28. Turn left on Rte. 28, drive to Chatham Center, and follow the rotary out of town on Rte. 28 toward Orleans. Inn is on left about ½ mile down road.

The guest bed chambers vary in atmosphere, from old fashioned Clarissa, *above,* to the formally elegant Hannah Rebekah, *right, above,* to the spacious colonial Hiram Harding suite, *below.*

WEDGEWOOD INN

Yarmouth Port   MASSACHUSETTS

The Cape Cod of yesteryear

The Old King's Highway, Route 6A, traverses Cape Cod Bay, passing through historic villages untouched by commercialism. It is along this stretch of road that visitors experience the soft spirit of the Cape.

The village of Yarmouth Port, which was an active seaport until the twentieth century, is located at the mid-point of this sandy crescent of land that sweeps into the sea. It was here, in 1812, that a successful maritime attorney built his handsome Greek Revival home close to the bustling harborside.

Today, Jeffrey and Jill Jackson own that home, and the Wedgewood Inn is a beautiful reflection of their pursuit of excellence. As the name implies, the inn carries out a theme of Wedgewood blue and, as a result, feels calm and elegant. The first-floor bedrooms are the most formal of the six, with handmade, cherry pencil-post bedsteads; comfortable wing and bow-back Windsor chairs; glistening long-leaf yellow pine floorboards; oil paintings; and working fireplaces. Each has a private, screened porch, which transforms the suites into idyllic summer retreats. Rooms on the second floor, two with working fireplaces, are cheering and a trifle less formal, with their colorful old quilts, painted floors, and sprightly wallpapers; and the third-floor bedroom, alone at the top of the house, offers a view of the bay across treetops.

A bit of thoughtful planning when the house was constructed allows each room a great deal of privacy, as none shares a common wall. This detail reinforces the Jacksons' commitment to guests' privacy.

Rather than a communal affair, breakfast is served at separate, linen-draped tables in the dining room.

Left: Wedgewood blue plays a prominent role throughout the inn, and the fireplaces add warmth and cheer to these second floor guest rooms.

French doors, a pewter chandelier, a bay window, and cabinets filled with Wedgewood and antique china create a warm mood. The morning's offerings include fresh-baked breads and fresh fruits, or a more exotic dish such as pears poached in wine or an apple or peach tart. With advance reservations, Saturday night guests can request a six-course dinner to be served at the inn. The Jacksons work with a fine local caterer, who designs each menu to fit the season.

WEDGEWOOD INN, 83 Main St., Rte. 6A, Yarmouth Port, MA 02675; (617) 362-5157; Jeffrey and Jill Jackson, Innkeepers. Rates: *moderate* to *expensive;* continental breakfast included. Open year round; 6 rooms in inn, all with private baths, some with shower or with tub only. No bar; guests may bring liquor. No children; no pets; Visa, MasterCard accepted. Two acres of gardens on premises; beach, marshlands, sightseeing, antiquing nearby.

DIRECTIONS: Take Rte. 6 (Mid-Cape Hwy.) to exit 6 (Willow St.). Turn right onto Willow toward Yarmouth Port and Rte. 6A. Turn right on Rte. 6A, which will lead to the inn on your right.

RALPH WALDO EMERSON INN
YANKEE CLIPPER INN

Rockport   **MASSACHUSETTS**

Two family inns on a picturesque cape

During World War II, when Fred Wemyss was in the army, his wife, Lydia, worked in Boston and spent weekends in Rockport with friends. When Fred returned from the war, Lydia brought him to Rockport. The couple bought a house and turned it into a country inn.

Thirty-eight years later, Fred and Lydia are the owners of a thriving country inn business in that historic old town they love so much. Consisting of three converted houses, the Yankee Clipper Inn is managed by the Wemysses' daughter, Barbara, and her husband, Bob Ellis. The Ralph Waldo Emerson Inn, a huge old white hotel down the street, is managed by their son, Gary, and his wife, June. Among the sixty-four rooms at the two inns, there is such a wide variety of accommodations and activities that almost everyone can find something to please.

At the Yankee Clipper complex, the prevailing theme is nautical. The Wemysses love the ocean and share their affection for it with guests at this seaside resort. Seafood is always on the menu in the Clipper

The hand-turned stairway in the Bullfinch House.

Left: The Yankee Clipper's furnishings come from all over the world.

Inn's glass-enclosed dining room. Guest rooms are named after clipper ships, and one, the Sovereign of the Seas Room, even has a porthole in the shower.

The inn, a Georgian mansion with saltwater pool, is the center of activity for the Yankee Clipper complex. Rooms vary in size and furnishings, but most are filled with antiques and provide oceanfront views.

Trekking through a flower garden, visitors come to The Quarter Deck, a more contemporary dwelling with eight attractive guest rooms, seven with huge picture windows facing the ocean—or more aptly, bordering on the ocean. The water appears to be right outside the window, and the thought of diving in to take a swim is tempting. Fred Wemyss likes to call the view his "landlubber's cruise"—"all of the ocean with none of the motion."

Across the street from these two buildings is the Bullfinch House, an 1840 Greek Revival home, named for its renowned architect and a favorite spot for visiting architects. The rooms are somewhat small, but the decorative lintels, delicate hand-turned stairway, multiple ceiling moldings, and numerous other architectural details have a special charm that more than compensates for any limitations in size. Some of the leaded-glass windows are slightly cracked, but Fred refuses to replace anything that might be of historic interest. One window, for instance, bears a woman's name etched with a diamond ring back in 1863.

Food at the Yankee Clipper Inn is good, downhome fare. "The staff cooks the way I want them to," says Fred, "Fannie Farmer and *Joy of Cooking*." The corn chowder, blueberry pancakes, zucchini bread, mock cheesecake, and baked scrod are delicious, as are the cranberry Bavarian mousse and fudge pies. Vegetables are generally fresh, and steamed lobsters are available most nights.

Over at the Ralph Waldo Emerson Inn, named for the great New England author who was a frequent guest, the atmosphere is a skillful blend of the old and new. The four-story white building is reminiscent of a large old hotel, with its high-ceilinged living room, old-fashioned bedrooms, and oversized porch. The oldest part of the building, an 1806 tavern, was moved to its present site in 1866, and a major section was added about fifty years later. On the contemporary side, the inn boasts a mini-movie theater, along with a sauna and whirlpool room that can be reserved by the hour.

There is a swimming pool in back and a large open area where you can enjoy the view of the ocean or watch the weekly sailboat races. Guest rooms tend to have a turn-of-the-century look, with globe lamps, glass door transoms, and soft pastel curtains. The

A guest room at the Ralph Waldo Emerson.

rooms are comfortable and airy, and all have private baths.

Meals are simple, with a daily meat and fish entrée and a special baked stuffed lobster. "People want to know if our lobster is from Maine," says Gary. "Sometimes they think they *are* in Maine. No, sir, I tell them. Everything here is from Sandy Bay."

He can be a bit chauvinistic, but since he has grown up in such a fascinating old town, he probably has a right to be. There is nothing like his inevitable retort to the baffled tourist. "When they want to know where they are, I tell them we're bordered by Gloucester on one side and Portugal on the other."

YANKEE CLIPPER INN, 127 Granite Street, Rockport, MA 01966; (617) 546-3407; Fred and Lydia Wemyss, Owners; Barbara and Bob Ellis, Innkeepers. Rates: *inexpensive* to *moderate*, with breakfast, lunch, and dinner, or just with breakfast; 15% service charge is additional. Open all year; 25 guest rooms spread over 3 buildings, all with private baths. Children over 3 welcome; no pets; no credit cards. Swimming pool; golf, sailing, boating, tennis nearby.

DIRECTIONS: From Boston take I-95 east from I-93 to Rte. 128 to Gloucester. Turn left at first set of traffic lights onto Rte. 127. Drive 5 miles to large intersection in Rockport, turn left again at sign for Pigeon Cove and Annisquam. Inn is on Rte. 127 at the ocean.

RALPH WALDO EMERSON INN, Cathedral Avenue, Rockport, MA 01966; (617) 546-6321; Gary and June Wemyss, Innkeepers. Rates: *inexpensive* including breakfast and dinner; European plan also available; 15% service charge additional. Open mid-May to end of Oct.; open weekends April through Nov.; 37 guest rooms with private baths. Children welcome (cribs available); no pets; no credit cards. Swimming pool, sauna, whirlpool, game room.

DIRECTONS: On Rte. 127 in Rockport, drive 2 miles beyond Yankee Clipper, turn right at inn sign, and drive to end of street.

The spacious lobby of the Ralph Waldo Emerson.

Right: Views at the Yankee Clipper.

COUNTRY INN AT PRINCETON

Princeton

MASSACHUSETTS

Find out what heaven is like

If eating delicious food in beautiful surroundings is your idea of heaven, a stay at the County Inn at Princeton should be added to your list of "musts." Innkeepers Don and Maxine Plumridge have set for themselves a demanding goal: to ensure their guests an unforgettable dining experience.

The setting for this late Victorian, gambrel-roofed "cottage," built in 1890 by Senator Charles G. Washburn, is definitely country; yet the inn is only fifty miles west of Boston. The house dominates a hilltop and affords a panoramic view of rolling Massachusetts woodlands and on clear nights, the lights of Boston.

Left: The stunning Chinese red in the tiny Library dining room is reflected in a wall of mirrors.

The Plumridges spared no expense in rejuvenating their grandly proportioned great house, whose first floor is especially luxurious. The living room, in rich and warm hues of blue, cream, and rose, is furnished with tufted Victorian settees, plush easy chairs, mounted trophies, and wildlife engravings. Here, or, in summer, on the expansive slate patio, dinner guests begin the evening. Over drinks, diners peruse the menu, order, and relax before a blazing fire or bask in the last light of day. When the first course is ready to serve, guests are guided to one of three beautifully appointed dining rooms and the feast begins. Though the chef changes the menu to reflect each season, a representative sampling of autumnal offerings gives an idea of the pleasures that await. Consider starting with a confit of quail and an apple-onion fritter served with a hot cider sauce seasoned with juniper, or Wellfleet oysters, napped with a champagne truffle sauce, and paired with sweet periwinkles and garnished with imported sea beans.

Wild game is a feature of the inn, both on the menu and on the walls.

Entrées are equally provocative. For example, one might choose from sautéed tenderloin of beef crowned with a roquefort-walnut compound butter and served with a grilled, ham-wrapped sweetbread and green tomato pickle; double-cut venison chops marinated in scotch, white wine, juniper, and herbs, grilled over mesquite, and served with a piquant stewed red cabbage and an apple-turnip puree; or loin of lamb stuffed with a goat cheese, sweet pepper, and rosemary mousse, served with a leek-and-fresh-artichoke flan, and accompanied by yellow and red bell pepper sauces. Formidable! To complete the pleasure, the Plumridges take care to see that the wine list complements the efforts of the chef. Soups, salads, and desserts, made fresh each day, are superb.

Sated with that delight only excellent food and wine can create, the fortunate diner stumbles upstairs to one of the inn's six spacious bedchambers. Each of the rooms is named for a wildflower, and with their mix of antiques and traditional furnishings, all carry out an informal country theme.

Right: Most guest rooms are over-sized and comfortable, and are filled with an eclectic mix of furnishings.

COUNTRY INN AT PRINCETON, 30 Mountain Rd., Princeton, MA 01541; (617) 464-2030; Don and Maxine Plumridge, Innkeepers. Rates: *expensive;* continental breakfast included. Open year round, but closed Mondays and Tuesdays; 6 parlour suites, all with private baths, some with showers only. Four-star gourmet dining room open Wednesday through Sunday to both inn guests and the public. No children, no pets; Visa, MasterCard, American Express accepted. Major ski facility, wildlife preserve, and Old Sturbridge Village nearby.

DIRECTIONS: From Connecticut and Massachusetts Tnpke., follow Rte. 290 north to Rte. 190. Take exit 5 (Rte. 140) and follow to Princeton. At Rte. 62, turn left and drive 4 miles. Turn right at post office and flashing light. Pass town common on left, and inn is 200 yards up Mountain Rd. on right.

A once-flourishing resort town, Princeton is filled with charming architecture.

A totally romantic inn, perfectly named

Magnificent cuisine in luxurious surroundings.

Off the beaten track in the lake country of Massachusetts, The Victorian attracts a wide and enthusiastic following by the sheer power of its beauty and the quality of its cuisine.

Built in 1871 as an elaborate private home for local gentry, the house was neglected for several years before innkeepers Orin and Martha Flint set about restoring this grand dame to its original glory. The exterior, painted a glowing salmon pink, is trimmed with fresh white decorative detailing: ornate balustrades; fretwork; pilasters; arched window moldings with bold keystones; and a diamond-patterned, fishscale, slate mansard roof. James Fletcher Whitin, for whom the house was constructed, spared no expense on the interior, commissioning artisans to fit his twenty-three-room mansion with rich wood paneling, intricate moldings, gilt valances, and exquisite chandeliers.

The first floor of the inn is devoted to dining in three rooms draped in opulent fabrics and colors, echoing the spirit of the Victorian age. Ornate floral wallcoverings, heavy brocade draperies, a creamy white marble mantel, a grand piano, and etched glass doors envelope the senses with warmth and opulence. The menu lives up to this luxurious décor, offering an interesting array of starters and main courses, such as a first course of shrimp and prosciutto vinaigrette, carpaccio—thin slices of raw sirloin dressed with oil, vinegar, and spices—and lobster served with a warm butter sauce on a chiffonade of romaine and mushrooms. Entrées include salmon poached in dill butter and bathed in cream and capers, boneless breast of duck with brandied peach sauce, and sautéed

Left: The inn's décor is almost legendary in its perfection, as this sumptuous dressing room in the main guest room illustrates.

veal on a bed of creamed onions napped with a port wine glaze. Old-fashioned and classic desserts such as *zuppa inglese,* chocolate comfort, and plum pudding are accompanied by the inn's selection of after-dinner coffees and liqueurs.

To reach the inn's guest rooms, one mounts the lustrous broad staircase to the upper stories of the house. Each bedchamber has an individual style, from the exotic Armour Room, with its heavily embossed wainscotting, bold wallpaper, and accent colors of green, wine, and black, to the River Room, a sophisticated garret in soft shades of raisin and taupe with art deco and oriental prints and a flashy papiermâché parrot standing guard in the bathroom.

THE VICTORIAN, 583 Linwood Ave., Whitinsville, MA 01588; (617) 234-2500; Orin and Martha Flint, Innkeepers. Rates: *moderate* to *expensive;* continental breakfast included. Open year round; 8 rooms, all with private baths; Dining room, open to the public, serves dinner daily, except Mondays; Sunday brunch. Children welcome; major credit cards accepted. Antiquing, spelunking, crafts shops, Old Sturbridge Village nearby.

DIRECTIONS: From north on Rte. 146, take Purgatory Chasm exit to Whitinsville. Turn right at traffic light in town center onto Linwood Ave. Inn is on left about 1 mile beyond center. From south on Rte. 146, take Uxbridge exit and go about 2 miles beyond Uxbridge traffic light on Rte. 121 to sign for Whitinsville. Turn left; inn is on right beyond mill pond.

Traditional feasting, modern comfort

The Publick House is a classic New England hostelry that dates back to 1771, when Colonel Ebenezer Crafts built this popular tavern on the common. Crafts was an energetic colonist who organized and equipped the Sturbridge militia and who trained his men on the tavern's front yard, the village green. He and his troops defended a beseiged Boston, an effort that won him the rank of colonel. Crafts would be both pleased and amazed to see how his Publick

Left: Yuletide festivities culminate in the Wassail Toast, the Boar's Head Procession, and lavish feasting.

House has grown and prospered over the years. Under the stewardship of gifted innkeeper Buddy Adler, the inn is a haven that offers comfort to travelers and leaves an afterglow of fond memories.

Best known, perhaps, for its bountiful Yankee victuals, the inn serves three full meals a day plus a late supper in the Tavern Room. A random sampling of Publick House specials must include lobster pie, chock full of succulent and lightly sauced meat; loin lamb chops cut so thick they have to be custom-butchered; tangy Indian pudding served hot with a mound of vanilla ice cream; and the inn's famous and mouthwatering pecan sticky buns. No matter the meal, dining at the Publick House is pure pleasure.

Rooms at the inn vary widely, from colonial bedrooms with sloping floorboards, open beamwork,

In Ebenezer Craft's day, meals were cooked in this enormous walk-in fireplace.

and a variety of antique and fine reproduction furniture, to spacious two-room suites in the neighboring Chamberlain House. Over the years the Publick House has grown considerably, and today it includes a bed-and-breakfast house, The Colonel Ebenezer Crafts Inn, located a little over a mile from the main inn, as well as a motor lodge and accompanying casual restaurant for travelers who opt for all the modern conveniences.

Sturbridge is the gateway to New England, and there is no better place to either begin or end a tour of the countryside than this historic town. To enrich one's understanding of colonial America, a visit to Old Sturbridge Village, a two-hundred-acre restored New England agricultural village, is a must. This is a living museum where the staff, dressed in authentic garb, carry on the toils of everyday colonial life.

PUBLICK HOUSE, on the Common, Sturbridge, MA 01566; (617) 347-3313: Buddy Adler, Innkeeper. Rates: *moderate* to *expensive*. Open year round; 20 rooms in Publick House, 5 in Chamberlain, 9 in Ebenezer Crafts Inn, and 100 in motor lodge, all with private baths, some with showers only. Restaurant, open to the public, serves three meals and a late supper daily. Children welcome; 1 pet per room in Publick House "at guests' risk;" all major credit cards accepted. Tennis, bicycling, swimming, running trails on premises; Old Sturbridge Village, antiquing, and sightseeing nearby.

DIRECTIONS: From Hartford, Conn., take I-84, which becomes I-86. Continue on I-86 to exit 33 (Sturbridge). From Albany or Boston, take Massachusetts Tnpke. to exit 9. Inn is on Sturbridge Common, Rte. 131.

The Pumpkin Room, *left,* is a private dining room. A gingerbread village, *right,* is made each year for the Yuletide festivities.

Upstairs, the guest rooms feature comfortable beds in a Colonial atmosphere with all of the modern amenities.

Historic Deerfield, one of America's treasures

Nestled in the verdant Connecticut River Valley lowlands, historic Deerfield is one of America's quiet treasures. Visitors enter this minute, tree-lined village to discover a serene and breathtaking avenue, exactly one mile long. On this street reside perfectly restored architectural gems dating to the mid-1700s, interspersed with the grounds and buildings of three fine boys' academies: Deerfield, Eaglebrook, and Bement. The group responsible for this bucolic "miracle mile"

PREVIOUS PAGE: Deerfield's mile-long main street is called merely The Street, and is shown here with an historic church and the Deerfield Inn. *Left:* the Dwight-Barnard House, circa 1725, one of the many restored buildings open to the public.

is the Heritage Foundation of Deerfield, formed by philanthropists Mr. and Mrs. Henry N. Flynt, who committed the foundation to the task of promoting an appreciation of the rich heritage of the early colonies, and to preserving the principles and standards of the early settlers.

Twelve impeccably furnished and maintained buildings are open to the public; the aggregate collection of paintings, furniture, silver, ceramics, tex-

One building of Deerfield Academy, the nation's premier prep school.

tiles, and decorative arts dispersed among the twelve is staggering in both quality and scope. In fact, so fine is the collection that Old Deerfield is considered a major muscum for the study of American culture.

Midway along the length of this historic lane, one finds the Deerfield Inn, a wonderful place to hang your hat while exploring the riches of the village. The inn, which suffered a devastating fire in 1979, reopened in 1981. This brand-new building conforms in every way to the spirit of Deerfield, while providing all of the comforts of a very good, small hotel. Each of the twenty-three guest rooms is furnished with lovely antiques and fine reproduction furniture, and the quality of fabrics used throughout the inn is stunning.

The inn's dining room, recently featured in *Gourmet* magazine, is committed to high standards of excellence. It offers abundant American fare, served with a sophisticated flair. Prime cuts of meat, fresh fish, and fowl are accompanied by the inn's homemade breads, garden-fresh native vegetables, palate-cleansing fresh fruit sorbets, and a rainbow of classic American desserts.

DEERFIELD INN, The Street, Deerfield, MA 01342; (413) 774-5587; Paul Burns, Innkeeper. Rates: *moderate*. Open year round, except Christmas Day; 23 rooms in inn, all with private bath. Restaurant, open to the public, serves lunch and dinner daily, except for Christmas Day; the coffee shop serves breakfast daily. Children and pets welcome; major credit cards accepted. Historic Deerfield, sightseeing, antiquing nearby.

DIRECTIONS: From New York City, take I-95 north to Hartford and then I-91 north to exit 24 (South Deerfield). Take Rte. 5/10 and follow signs for Historic Deerfield. From Boston, take Rte. 2 west to Greenfield and then Rte. 5/10 five miles to Deerfield.

The Street is lined with many beautiful private homes, as shown in these three photographs.

Lenox # VILLAGE INN **MASSACHUSETTS**

As much personality as a person

The parlor is filled with family heirlooms.

"I think a house can have as much personality as a person. The first time I stepped into this inn, I immediately felt its warm vibrations," remembers Innkeeper Cliff Rudisill, who isn't alone in enjoying the fine patina of The Village Inn. Built in 1771 as a farmhouse, the inn today is comprised of the main house and two adjoining, slate-roofed barns that years ago were converted into guest rooms. The village of Lenox "filled out" over two centuries and grew around the inn, which is located on a side street in the village proper.

The first floor of the inn offers guests a choice of comfortable common areas, including a large, screened-in porch filled with wicker furniture and surrounded by peony bushes and climbing vines.

Several years ago Cliff and his partner, Ray Wilson, toured the British Isles in search of the definitive English tea. After sampling dozens and researching the subject thoroughly, they returned with a superior recipe for scones and a method for making rich clotted cream. Each day from 3:30 to 5:00 The Village Inn offers an authentic tea, and once a month the inn orchestrates a "high tea," complete with chamber music and the requisite hot savory.

Guest rooms come in a wide variety of sizes, and several boast their own working fireplaces. Each of the rooms has that rustic and irregular charm that harks back to a colonial heritage. But before succumbing to a good night's sleep, one should enjoy dinner at the inn. Cliff and Ray take great pride in their dinner menu, which features such succulent specialties as pecan-breaded chicken breast served with a Dijon mustard sauce; pork loin with a port wine, prune, orange zest, ginger, and walnut sauce; and poached salmon with ginger Hollandaise sauce.

Room 23, with its pencil post bed and fireplace, is one of the inn's special guest chambers.

Left: Authentic English tea with freshly baked scones and clotted cream is served every afternoon.

THE VILLAGE INN, 16 Church St., Lenox, MA 01240; (413) 637-0020; Clifford Rudisill and Ray Wilson, Innkeepers. Rates: *moderate* to *expensive.* Open year round; 27 rooms, most with private baths. Breakfast served daily; dinner served Wednesday through Sunday; dining room open to the public. No pets; MasterCard, Visa accepted.

DIRECTIONS: From New York City, take the Taconic Pkwy. to Hillsdale (Rte. 23) exit. Follow Rte. 23 east to Great Barrington and Rte. 7. Turn left on Rte. 7 and continue through Stockbridge. At first traffic light past Stockbridge, turn left on Rte. 7A and continue into Lenox.

Great dining inspired by Albert Stockli

The Federal House is a classic example of the "overnight success" that is founded upon years of hard work and attention to detail. Innkeepers Robin Slocum and Ken Almgren met when they worked at the renowned Stonehenge restaurant in Ridgefield, Connecticut. Like ducks to water, both Robin and Ken took to the stringent rules of fine European service and they decided that one day they would have their own restaurant.

By 1982 Robin and Ken, who had married in the intervening years, found this stately home on the banks of the scenic Housatonic River. Two months after the purchase, they opened a European-style inn and restaurant that reflects their years of training and experience.

Guests enter the foyer of The Federal House to discover three dining rooms adorned with white damask, heavy silver, and fresh flowers. To capitalize on fresh foods the Almgrens change their menu three times a year. In autumn the emphasis is on game and might include fresh rabbit, venison, partridge, or goose. The spring menu takes full advantage of young lamb and seasonal fish, while in summer the chef features an array of cold appetizers and a generally lighter fare. No matter the season, the menu always offers several varieties of fish as well as veal, poultry, beef, and lamb.

The second floor of the inn is the private domain

Each of the three dining rooms is dressed in damask, silver, and fresh flowers.

of the Almgrens' overnight guests. Bedchambers are fresh and furnished with a light hand. For example, Room One is an old-fashioned charmer with angled ceiling, painted wood-slat wall boards, lustrous pine plank floor, and braided area rugs. Room Seven is bathed with a light that emanates from plush seafoam green carpet, white-on-white bed linens, white furniture, and white wallpaper delicately patterned with floral sprays. A massive gilt mirror adds a note of drama and weight to this bright and cheering room.

The entry hall creates the mood of a French country inn.

Left: The elegant, pillared porch of the soft red-brick inn faces the Housatonic River.

THE FEDERAL HOUSE, Rte. 102, South Lee, MA 01260; (413) 243-1824; Robin Slocum Almgren and Kenneth Almgren, Innkeepers. Rates: *moderate* to *expensive;* full breakfast included. Open 11 months of the year; closed 1 month in spring; 7 rooms, all with private baths or showers. Breakfast served daily to inn guests; dinner served daily, except Tuesdays, to inn guests and the public. No children under 12; no pets. MasterCard, Visa accepted. Golf and tennis at a nearby club.

DIRECTIONS: From New York City, take the Taconic Pkwy. to Hillsdale (Rte. 23) exit. Take Rte. 23 to Rte. 7 and turn left on Rte. 7, following it to Stockbridge. Turn right onto Main St. in Stockbridge (Rte. 102) and drive 1½ miles to inn.

RED LION INN

Stockbridge   **MASSACHUSETTS**

A fabled inn in an historic town

Tucked away in the very heart of the Berkshire Mountains, The Red Lion Inn is a landmark that offers comfort to tired wayfarers and serves as the hub of local activity. Its wide veranda is furnished with comfortable rocking chairs and cushioned settees that beckon for a leisurely hour of easy conversation, people watching, and sipping a favorite beverage. The inn, which has been in continuous use since the late 1700s, dominates the Main Street of tiny Stockbridge, a charming and historic New England village comprised of inviting shops, museums, a summer theater, and white clapboard manor houses. Perhaps the best-known resident of Stockbridge was painter Norman Rockwell, who lived around the corner from the inn and used Stockbridge residents as models for his paintings. Many famous Rockwell prints adorn guest room walls.

The lobby of the Red Lion is especially welcoming. Its broad expanse is filled with a happy warmth created by people perusing menus, meeting with long-lost relatives or friends, or simply reading a newspaper before a crackling fire. A stunning collection of antique furniture and china—a collection that dates back to the mid-1800s—is in fine repair and fills all

four floors of the inn. And the Red Lion is always filled with fresh flowers, for which owner Jane Fitzpatrick has a special love.

Guest rooms come in a variety of shapes and sizes. The neighboring Stafford House offers luxurious two-room suites, while in the main building there are both spacious one-room bedchambers "done up" with queen-size, four-poster beds, plush carpets, and deluxe fabrics as well as smaller, old-fashioned, share-a-bath bedrooms.

The Red Lion serves classic American food, including prime ribs of beef, double lamb chops, roast Long Island duckling, poached salmon, chicken pot pie, and Yankee pot roast. Desserts are equally all-American, ranging from apple pie with cheddar cheese or ice cream to Indian pudding. The inn's newly redecorated Lion's Den bistro offers diners a light evening fare of homemade soups, dinner salads, and overstuffed sandwiches, accompanied by live entertainment.

Corner suite, with Victorian antiques.

Left: Three antique teapots from the inn's vast collection of china and pewter. OVERLEAF: *Left, above,* part of the building's rear façade; *below,* gourds decorate the sideboard beneath a German winter landscape in the dining room. *Right,* a porch retreat with a seasonal motif.

THE RED LION INN, Stockbridge, MA 01262; (413) 298-5545; John and Jane Fitzpatrick, Owners; Betsy Holtzinger, Innkeeper. Rates: *moderate* to *expensive*. Open year round; 105 rooms in inn, including suites; 3 separate houses; private and shared baths, some with showers only. Dining room open daily to inn guests and the public for breakfast, lunch, and dinner. Children welcome; no pets; all major credit cards accepted. Heated swimming pool; live entertainment nightly in Lion's Den Pub; meeting rooms available for business. Tennis, golf, skiing nearby.

DIRECTIONS: From New York City, take the Taconic Pkwy. to Hillsdale (Rte. 23) exit. Drive east on Rte. 23 to Rte. 7. Turn left onto Rte. 7 and drive to Stockbridge's Main St. Inn is on the corner of Rte. 7 and Main St. From Boston, take the Massachusetts Tnpke. to exit 2. Turn left and follow Rte. 7 to inn on Main St. in Stockbridge.

WHEATLEIGH

An Italian palazzo in the Berkshires

One of the most attractive guest rooms.

"We are not a quaint little New England inn," laughed innkeeper and master of understatement Susan Simon as we strolled through the grand proportions of Wheatleigh. Styled after a sixteenth-century palazzo, Wheatleigh was built at the turn of the century by a wealthy American industrialist as a wedding present for his daughter, who married a Spanish count (she was forevermore known as "The Countess"). From the wrought iron and glass canopy over the grand entryway to the exquisite fixtures in each spacious marble-and-tile bathroom, no expense was spared to create a place of luxury and style.

Both Susan and Lin Simon have an abiding interest in the arts, an interest reflected in the many pieces of modern sculpture displayed throughout the first floor. Their love of art is also expressed in Wheatleigh's intimate restaurant. The Simons' goal is to maintain a fine restaurant in the Berkshires, and many patrons say they've arrived; entrées might feature veal, beef, and reindeer filets bourguignon or pheasant with morel sauce.

Wheatleigh sits on the crest of a hill and offers a beautiful view of the Stockbridge Bowl, a view enjoyed from many of the guest bedrooms. The bedchambers are individually decorated, and they range in size from tiny to expansive. No matter the accommodation, all guests share in the surpassing elegance and charm of this extraordinary mansion, its spacious grounds, and secluded swimming pool.

Hallway to the first-floor guest rooms.

Left: Two elegantly proportioned stained-glass windows filter soft summer light onto the main staircase.
OVERLEAF: The south terrace of Wheatleigh.

WHEATLEIGH, P.O. Box 824, Lenox, MA 01240; (413) 637-0610; Linfield and Susan Simon, Innkeepers. Rates: *expensive.* Open year round; 17 rooms, all with private baths, some with showers only. Dining room, open to the public, serves breakfast daily and dinner 6 days a week. Children over 8 welcome; no pets. All major credit cards accepted. Swimming pool and tennis court on premises; sports, shopping, and cultural events nearby.

DIRECTIONS: From New York City, take the Taconic Pkwy. to Hillsdale (Rte. 23) exit. Drive east on Rte. 23 to Rte. 7 and turn left to Stockbridge. In Stockbridge, cross Main St. (Rte. 102) and continue straight up hill 5 miles to the inn. From Boston, take Massachusetts Tnpke. to exit 2. Bear left on Rte. 102 and drive through Stockbridge. Immediately past The Red Lion Inn, turn right and drive up the hill 5 miles to the inn.

WEATHERVANE INN

South Egremont   MASSACHUSETTS

The comfortable main parlor.

Warm and homey in any season

The Weathervane Inn resides at the edge of scenic South Egremont, a tranquil New England village listed on the National Register of Historic Places. Innkeepers Anne and Vincent Murphy, and their daughter, Patricia, are congenial hosts whose enthusiasm for innkeeping is genuine and infectious.

The inn, a 1785 colonial structure, is a rambling two-story affair that feels more like a family home than a public hostelry, though it has served as an inn and/or general store since it was built. The first floor houses two dining rooms, one with bow windows that face the village and a second, newer room that looks out over the inn's swimming pool toward the adjoining golf course. Both breakfast and dinner are included in the price of a room and Anne's cooking is superior; she is particularly proud of her lemon chicken parmesan and butterflied leg of lamb.

Guest rooms are found on the second floor of the inn. Each has a character all its own and all are comfortably furnished with Early American reproductions. In a separate cottage on the grounds are two simple suites, one with complete kitchenette.

The Weathervane is a very warm and homey spot. During the Tanglewood season the Murphys will pack a gourmet picnic to be savored on the lawn before a concert. During fall and winter, guests' favorite activity after a long day in the Berkshires entails fixing a drink at the honor bar and settling in to watch a movie on the inn's tape machine. Or they might ask for Vince to spin a few tales—his long career as a private investigator in Manhattan sparks the imagination!

Each guest room feels old fashioned and comfortable.

WEATHERVANE INN, Rte. 23, P.O. Box 388, South Egremont, MA 01258; (413) 528-9580; Anne and Vincent Murphy and Patricia Murphy, Innkeepers. Rates: *moderate* to *expensive;* breakfast and dinner included. Open year round, except first 3 weeks in April; 6 rooms in main house, 2 in coach house; all with private baths, one with shower only. Dining room serves breakfast daily and dinner daily except Tuesdays; open to the public by reservation. Children discouraged; no pets; MasterCard, Visa, Diners Club accepted. Swimming pool and antiques shop on premises; Egremont Country Club, golf, tennis, and antiquing nearby.

DIRECTIONS: From New York City, take the Saw Mill River Pkwy. to Taconic Pkwy. to Hillsdale (Rte. 23) exit. Turn right on Rte. 23 and follow to South Egremont. From Boston, take Massachusetts Tnpke. to Lee exit, and Rte. 102 to Stockbridge. Take Rte. 7 south to Great Barrington to Rte. 23 west. Inn is 3 miles west on Rte. 23.

North Egremont

ELM COURT INN

A dining table laden with irresistable dishes

Since its beginnings as a tavern in 1790, Elm Court Inn has offered hearty and delicious food to road-weary travelers and locals alike. The philosophy of innkeepers Catherine and Joseph Mueller is to present their guests with abundant, high-quality fare, served piping hot and very fresh. The only complaint ever issued by guests is that the dining table is *too* laden with irresistible dishes.

Joseph became an apprentice chef at age fourteen in his native Switzerland, and the menu, neatly presented on a large chalkboard, reflects his Swiss heritage and continental training. Before ordering, diners enjoy the inn's savory homemade pâté served in an earthenware crock. Raclette, a Swiss dish made with melted cheese, is a favorite first course, as is smoked trout with horseradish sauce, and escargot Café de Paris. Wiener schnitzel, veal Parisienne, broiled sweetbreads with herb butter, duck à l'orange, calves brains in black butter, chicken curry, and hassenpfeffer made from fresh local rabbit appear most every night, and each meal is accompanied by two fresh vegetables, a crisp salad, and buttery rosti, the Swiss version of hash browns.

The Elm Court doesn't advertise its overnight accommodations. Nonetheless, the six bedrooms above the restaurant attract quite a following. Though not filled with fancy furnishings, each chamber is immaculate and comfortable and offers a superior value for budget-minded inngoers. The inn's location, central to all the activities in the Berkshire Mountains, is simply grand.

ELM COURT INN, Rte. 71, North Egremont, MA 01252; (413) 528-0325; Catherine and Joseph Mueller, Innkeepers. Rates: *inexpensive;* continental breakfast included. Open April through February; 6 rooms in inn, with private and shared baths. Dining room, open to the public, serves dinner nightly, except Tuesdays, May through October; November through February is closed both Tuesdays and Wednesdays. Children welcome; no pets; no credit cards.

DIRECTIONS: From New York City, take the Taconic Pkwy. to Rte. 23/Hillsdale exit. Stay on Rte. 23 through South Egremont to Rte. 71 and turn left and follow to inn.

The chef's Swiss heritage is reflected in the menu and the décor.

WILLIAMSVILLE INN

West Stockbridge   **MASSACHUSETTS**

Escape life's daily grind

The Berkshire hills of western Massachusetts are renowned for their soft beauty and have long provided the perfect haven for artists, lovers of nature, and people escaping life's daily grind. One of its finest hideaways is the Williamsville Inn which is owned and operated by innkeepers Carl and Elizabeth Atkinson.

The inn resides along a shaded country road and encompasses a rambling white clapboard farmhouse and a separate renovated barn. Built in 1797 by gentleman farmer Christopher French, the black-shuttered inn is warmed by lustrous wide-plank pine floorboards that glow with a fine patina. Guest rooms, each named after a Berkshire resident from the past, vary in size and atmosphere. The Edna St. Vincent Millay room is a charming and rustic chamber with a plank-beamed, slanted ceiling; dark burgundy floral wallpaper; an antique Victorian bedstead; and a marble-topped vanity illuminated by an antique lamp. A small bowl of potpourri, assorted reading material, and two wing chairs add charm and comfort to this snug and private abode. The Christopher French room is located at the front of the inn. It served as the original owner's private bedchamber, and its working fireplace, antique hand-braided rugs, and a pencil post canopy bed resonate its colonial heritage.

One of the most special bedrooms is the Louisa May Alcott, found at the very top of the house on the third floor. Here, extra-wide, mellow pine floorboards are washed by soft light from the ceiling skylight window. The inn's large central chimney passes through the room forming a brick-walled alcove that contains one of the rooms two beds. Braided scatter rugs, comfortable reading chairs, a hassock, and books by Miss Alcott tempt visitors to linger long in this treetop retreat.

Located on the first floor are the inn's comfortable and beautifully furnished public rooms. The intimate tavern room sports newly stenciled walls, decorations created by two professional stencilers, who were guests at the inn. Passing out of the tavern and

Left: The Louisa May Alcott suite at the top of the house invites guests to linger.

The Tavern Room.

through the elegant formal parlor, guests enter the Garden Room. This well-equipped and comfortable "recreation center" contains great expanses of glass that offer a fine view of the inn's ten acres of woods and manicured lawn.

The dining room of The Williamsville Inn has gained a fine reputation over the years. The inn's talented chef, who specializes in country French cuisine prepared with an American touch, produces inventive and savory dishes based on the finest ingredients available throughout each season.

THE WILLIAMSVILLE INN, Route 41, West Stockbridge, Mass. 01266; (413) 274-6580; Carl and Elizabeth Atkinson, Innkeepers. Rates: *moderate.* Open all year, except first 3 weeks in Nov. and 3 weeks in April; 14 guest rooms with private baths. Children over 10 welcome; no pets; Visa, MasterCard accepted. Breakfast available. No lunch served.

DIRECTIONS: From New York City, take Sawmill River Pkwy. to Taconic Pkwy., exit at Hillsdale and take Rte. 23 east through Great Barrington to Rte. 41 north. Inn is 5 miles north on the left. From Boston, take Mass. Turnpike West to exit 1. Turn left on Rte. 41 south and continue 5 miles to inn on right.

CONNECTICUT

New Preston

BOULDERS INN

CONNECTICUT

A handsomely rustic, thoroughly inviting inn

The focal point of the living room at the Boulders Inn is a broad picture window, which offers a panoramic view of Lake Waramaug. As the name of the inn suggests, it is a lodge house constructed of timbers and massive boulders, finished with weathered shingles and dark green shutters. Rather than develop the rustic personality of the building, innkeepers Jim and Carolyn Woollen chose to decorate in a lighter vein, creating a homey feel. The living room is filled with groupings of chairs and couches. Crewelwork-upholstered wing chairs face each other in front of the windows, as do two Victorian sofas in front of the hearth. A cream colored couch looks out toward the water, and easy chairs in jewel shades of ruby and sapphire form conversation nooks. Rich wood paneling and a gleaming staircase add to the warmth of the scene. The total effect is handsome and thoroughly inviting.

The dining room is located just off the living room. It is quite large and is lit with Japanese rice paper lanterns that glow like matching full moons. The newest addition to the dining room is a circular bay with large wraparound windows that face both lake and woods and entertain diners with changes of season and weather. In summertime the inn serves three meals a day; during the leisurely days of winter

Boulders, for which the inn is named, appear prominently in the dining room.

a regular Sunday brunch attracts a loyal following. The evening meal is composed of traditional fare and inventive dishes. A sampling from the menu includes shrimp with artichoke hearts, boned duck breast with a tangy red wine and shallot sauce, veal with lemon and capers, tender morsels of lamb in a delicate curry, and a selection of broiled steaks and chops.

Accommodations are found on the second floor of the inn proper and in four independent cottages that sit on the sloping wooded hillside behind the inn. In the main house rooms are furnished with antiques, with a few traditional chairs or sofas added for guests' comfort. The independent cottages are simply furnished; many have fireplaces stocked and ready to light, and all have private balconies facing the lake.

The newest addition is the circular dining room.

PREVIOUS PAGE: Lake Waramaug seen from the Boulders Inn. *Left,* the staircase to the second floor guest rooms is particularly striking.

BOULDERS INN, Rte. 45, New Preston, CT 06777; (203) 868-7918; Carolyn and Jim Woollen, Innkeepers. Rates: *moderate* to *expensive.* Open year round, except for 2 weeks after Thanksgiving and 2 weeks in March; 5 rooms in inn, 8 rooms in cabins, all with private bath, some with showers only. Dining room, open to the public by reservation, serves three meals daily from Memorial Day to Labor day; after Labor Day, serves breakfast and dinner, but closed several nights a week. Children over 6 welcome; no pets; Visa, MasterCard accepted. Boating, swimming, tennis, bicycling, hiking on premises; horseback riding, downhill and cross-country skiing, antiquing, and summer theater nearby.

DIRECTIONS: From New York City, take Sawmill River Pkwy. or Hutchinson River Pkwy. to Rte. 684 north to I-84. Stay on I-84 to Rte. 7 north (exit 7), and take Rte. 7 to Rte. 202 in New Milford. Stay on Rte. 202 to New Preston. Turn left on Rte. 45 to the inn.

Austrian flair on a Connecticut lake

The country around Lake Waramaug has the look of long cultivation and use, but it hasn't been overrun by houses or bathing beaches. There are splendid views of the lake from the porches of the Hopkins Inn and from the large stone terrace at its side, as well as from several of its old-fashioned guest rooms, with their floral wallpapers, smoky mirrors, wicker chairs and white-painted woodwork. The view isn't the sole reason for the inn's popularity, however. Guests come primarily to dine.

Innkeeper and chef, Franz Schober is Austrian. His is a cuisine without a hint of excess, except perhaps in the texture of such dishes as calves brains au beurre noir. The spicing of the Wiener schnitzel and the roast pork paprika is handled with European discretion. The offerings are seasonal—poached salmon in summer, plentiful game in fall. Among the beautifully presented appetizers is a light liver pâté with a distinctive flavor. Prosciutto and melon make a wonderful start for a summer luncheon, which might continue with spinach salad or chicken Cordon Bleu. The Hopkins Inn pulls out all the stops with its rich desserts—a smooth white-chocolate mousse, meringue glacé and a variety of sundaes.

The day's dishes are announced on a slate brought to the table by a smiling waitress in dirndl skirt and peasant blouse. In warm weather, luncheon and dinner are served on the terrace. Indoors, there are two delightful dining rooms. One, with a view of the lake, has fanciful Austrian chandeliers and chairs in the Early American style. The other is darkly paneled and has the feel of a Gasthaus. Its marvelous fireplace is faced with figured tiles depicting the story of Rip Van Winkle in vibrant, earthy colors.

A foyer leads to the inn's bar, in the oldest portion of the building, an eighteenth-century farmhouse. The main part of the inn is a blocky, ample Greek Revival house with cupola, built in the 1840s by George C. Hopkins. The décor of its parlors still echoes the taste of the Victorian era, with curved sofas, overstuffed chairs, marble-topped tables and floral prints. After dinner, little more is needed to complete the evening than a stroll around the porch and grounds. Then to bed, drifting off to sleep to the sound of leaves rustling gently in the maples and the water lapping the shore of the lake below.

American décor contrasts with the Austrian Room beyond.

Left: Summer luncheon on the terrace at the Hopkins is a local tradition.

THE HOPKINS INN, New Preston, CT 06777; (203) 868-7295; Franz and Beth Schober, Innkeepers. Rates: *inexpensive.* Open May through Oct.; 9 guest rooms, 7 with private baths, 2 sharing, and 1 suite sleeping 3, with kitchenette, available Easter to New Years. Restaurant open Tuesday through Sunday, April to Jan., serving full breakfast and continental dinner; luncheon served during the season. Children welcome (cribs or cots available); no pets; no credit cards. Private beach on Lake Waramaug.

DIRECTIONS: From New York City, take Sawmill River Pkwy. to I-684. Follow to I-84 east to US-7/202 north. Where they divide at New Milford, take US-202 north to New Preston and turn left on Rte. 45. Past Lake Waramaug take first left and second right to inn.

Each guest room is prettier than the last

Built in 1745 as a private home for Captain William Bull, the Toll Gate Hill Inn is a large, gambrel-roofed, red clapboard colonial structure. After the Revolution, Bull's home became an inn, but never has it served that purpose so well as in its latest incarnation.

Though the entire inn underwent a major restoration in 1983, it remains true to its origins. Guests enter by way of the rustic tavern room, whose fireplace wood paneling are original to the house. The exquisite cherry wood bar was designed to match the paneling, and during the winter guests enjoy eating hot chestnuts grilled over the open hearth.

It is difficult to choose a favorite among the inn's six bedrooms, for one is prettier than the last. On the second floor are found three large and lovely suites with working fireplaces and sitting areas. Three

Left: The Ballroom dining room is beautifully proportioned.

smaller rooms on the third floor are equally charming. Eaved ceilings and exposed beams pair up with antique bedsteads and comfortable chairs, all dressed in a palette of lush and cheerful colors.

Innkeeper Fritz Zivic is working to make the Toll Gate's kitchen the finest in the area, and his chef reflects America's newly blossomed romance with indigenous foodstuffs. The inn offers grilled meats and fresh fish as well, and the wine cellar, though small, is discriminating.

TOLL GATE HILL INN, US-202 and Tollgate Rd., Litchfield, CT 06759; (203) 482-6116; Frederick J. Zivic, Innkeeper. Rates: *moderate*; continental breakfast included. Open year round; 6 rooms in inn, 12 to be available in annex by late summer 1985. Dining room, open to the public, serves lunch and dinner daily. Children welcome; well-behaved pets welcome; Visa, MasterCard, American Express accepted. Golf, horseback riding, boating, downhill and cross-country skiing, sightseeing, and antiquing nearby.

DIRECTIONS: From New York City, take I-87 to I-284 east to I-684 north. Continue on I-684 to I-84 east, and take I-84 to Rte. 7 north. Follow Rte. 7 to US-202 in New Milford and stay on 202 to Litchfield. Inn is on the left 2¼ miles past the Litchfield village green on US-202.

Room 3, with its paneled fireplace wall, has a wonderfully fresh look.

Reflecting the rich history of bygone days

Northeastern Connecticut recalls an idyllic pastoral painting depicting tranquil lakes, rolling mountains, bosky dells, and winding country roads. The inhabitants of the area take pride in meticulously maintaining their venerable old homes and spacious lawns, which add great character and charm to this rural scene. In the heart of this soft and welcoming countryside is the village of Salisbury and at its center, the White Hart Inn.

The original white clapboards and wide porches that surround the inn echo its beginnings as a farmhouse in the 1780s. By the mid-1800s, when the road passing by had become a much-traveled stagecoach route, the White Hart became an inn. Turn-of-the-century train travel transformed the northern reaches of Connecticut into a haven for wealthy city dwellers who flocked to the inn in summer and fall.

On the main floor visitors enjoy shopping in a country store filled with bright and cheerful gift items and delectable bakery goods prepared in the inn's own kitchen. Across the lobby, the Hunt Room, a newly renovated club room complete with upholstered wing chairs, working fireplace, wood paneled bar, and grand piano, is a stylish hideaway.

Guest rooms in the inn might be decorated with old fashioned English floral print draperies and period furniture or with more contemporary "American country" fabrics and wall coverings. Many guests choose to lodge in the clutch of attractive, attached motel-like units at the rear of the main inn—each with its own separate entrance—or in the luxurious, two-room Ethan Allen suite in the adjoining Gideon Smith House.

As a full-service inn, the White Hart offers three full meals every day of the year as well as an around-the-clock front desk service. Besides the inn's facilities, the area is filled with delightful restaurants, interesting shops, historic villages, nature trails, and sports centers, all of which makes for a varied and satisfying visit during any season of the year.

The country store is just off the lobby.

Left: The White Hart's namesake gazes over the inn's lobby.

WHITE HART INN, The Village Green, Salisbury, CT 06068; (203) 435-2511; Susan G. Redmond, General Manager, Joy Martorell, Assistant Manager. Rates: *moderate.* Open year round; 20 rooms in inn, 7 in neighboring Gideon Smith House, all with private baths, some with tub only. Dining room, open to the public, serves 3 meals daily. Children welcome; pets discouraged; Visa, MasterCard, American Express accepted.

DIRECTIONS: From I-684, go north to Millerton, N.Y., then east on Rte. 44 to inn at junction of Rte. 41 in Salisbury.

Ridgefield

THE ELMS

A sophisticated family carrying on established traditions

When you yearn for the look and ambience of a New England village, consider Ridgefield. All the elements are there, including fine old houses and majestic churches, reminders of a time when private property and public pride went hand in hand. The buildings of The Elms stand on ample grounds across from a town park. Built in the 1760s by master cabinetmaker Amos Seymour, the house became an inn in 1799. With its array of antiques, newly renovated annex, elegant four-posters, and white modern baths, the inn combines the comforts and conveniences of today with the charm and dignity of yesterday.

To local residents, The Elms is as comfortable and familiar as a club, and visitors from the city retreat here to country pleasures. While the prize guest rooms are those with vaulted ceilings and fireplaces created from the old ballroom upstairs, all twenty antiques-filled rooms in the inn hold special treasures.

The Elms is the pride of innkeepers Robert Scala and his sister-in-law Violet Scala, whose late husband Mario developed an exquisite cuisine that son Edward now maintains. The wide-ranging menu includes tournedos Helder, Chateaubriand, veal in champagne batter, quail in season, and a heavenly curry of sliced capon with chutney, coconut, and kumquats. Desserts are equally delectable: sherry-laced zabaglione, for example, is garnished with strawberries and served in long stemmed glasses, while peach flambé au brandy is definitely intoxicating!

The inn frequently finds occasion to celebrate—a morel party heralds a new shipment of the marvelous mushrooms; a January sanglier keeps alive the traditional New Year's feast of wild boar, also offering guests such treats as filet of sole Dieppoise and gâteau St. Honoré. A proper selection of wine is always

Once a ballroom, now a guest room.

available; Bobby Scala is especially proud of his extensive and carefully stocked wine cellar, which includes rare vintages. As long as there is a Scala to raise a glass with, the enchantment and warm spirit of The Elms will never lapse.

THE ELMS, 500 Main Street, Ridgefield, CT 06877; (203) 438-2541; Violet Scala and Robert Scala, Innkeepers. Rates: *moderate,* except for Bridal Chamber and Suite. Open all year; 20 guest rooms each with private bath, air conditioning, color TV and telephone. Dining room, open to public, renowned for haute cuisine and vintage wines; serves superlative lunch and dinner, Sunday brunch, and continental breakfast (for guests only). Dining room closed Wednesdays. Children welcome; no pets; Visa, MasterCard, American Express, Diners Club accepted. Public golf course and swimming nearby.

DIRECTIONS: From New York City, take Major Deegan to I-287 to I-684 north. At exit 6 take Rte. 35 east 12 miles to Ridgefield. Inn is on the right past third light, across from Ballard Park.

The library and sitting room.

Dine on dishes fit for a king

Named after the ancient Druid ruins which sit mysteriously on England's Salisbury Plain, Stonehenge is an inn that gladly yields its own mysteries to any traveler who cares to make the short trek to colonial Ridgefield.

Low-lying cottages form a complex around an old farmhouse, where a pine-paneled dining room upholds all the best traditions of fine dining. In the bar, there are enough old prints and dark corners to make even the most urban guest feel like a country squire just in from the hunt. A window in the wall provides a view of the wine cellar, which houses a collection of extraordinary vintages.

Of all the dining entrées that deserve such fine wines, one must be mentioned because it has to be ordered at least five days in advance—whole roast suckling pig, an exotic dish that is usually set only before kings, and quite a rarity at country inns. Less regal, but equally enticing fare consists of boneless breast of duck with calvados sauce, tournedos with wild rice, roast baby pheasant with wild mushrooms, saddle of venison with spiced crabapple and hunting lodge sauce, paté-stuffed roast quail with truffles in a red wine sauce, and Norwegian poached salmon. Aside from the usual Chateaubriand and roast rack of lamb, both excellently prepared, there is a Saturday night special, filet of beef Wellington with perigourdine sauce, that is worth looking forward to.

The perfect place for a romantic meal, Stonehenge also offers a more than ordinary overnight stay. The guest rooms are spacious and studded with antiques. Opened in 1947 by the legendary chef, Albert Stockli, Stonehenge was one of the first inns of its kind to be compared favorably with the best in Europe. Today, Stonehenge continues in that fine tradition.

Guest room in the Main House.

Left: The man-made falls and pond at Stonehenge. OVER-LEAF: the inn, with its idyllic mill pond.

STONEHENGE, P.O. Box 667, Rte. 7, Ridgefield, CT 06877; (203) 438-6511; David Davis and Douglas Seville, Innkeepers. Rates: *moderate;* continental breakfast included. Open all year except Tuesdays; 8 guest rooms, 3 master bedrooms, 2 suites, each with private bath, air conditioning, telephone, and cable color TV. Lunch and dinner, featuring superb continental cuisine, is served in 3 dining rooms overlooking the duck pond. Dining rooms closed Tuesdays. Children welcome (rollaway cots and cribs available); no pets; Visa, MasterCard, American Express, Diners Club accepted. Swimming pool.

DIRECTIONS: From New York City take Merritt Parkway to exit 40 onto Rte. 7 north. Inn is 13 miles north on the left side.

A living legacy of great popularity

The Silvermine Tavern sits at the edge of a tranquil mill pond side-by-side with an old mill dating to the Revolutionary era. The mirror-like pond is inhabited by long-necked swans and wild ducks, and the surrounding forest adds to the stillness of the setting. Though the inn is on the corner of a centuries-old crossroads dating back to the founding of the community of Silvermine, no sidewalks intrude upon this reposeful scene. Civilization feels far removed—that is, until stepping inside this vibrant, seventeenth-century tavern.

The Silvermine attracts diners from miles around because of its warm atmosphere and consistently fine food. Innkeepers Frank Whitman, Jr., and his father, Frank, Sr., who have owned the Silvermine since the 1950s, lavish constant love and attention on their inn. From a single structure, the original tavern grew over the years to encompass six dining rooms and an open-air deck shaded by trees towering up through the deck's floorboards. The mill pond and its rushing waterfall flow just below the deck and cast a romantic spell.

Each of the interior dining rooms is a museum of American arts and crafts, displaying a king's ransom in colonial tools, toys, woodenware, and portraits. Silvermine house specialties are many and abundant. Favorites include roast duckling served with apple cider sauce and an apple pecan dressing; succulent Maine lobster in a tender pie crust, stuffed with Silvermine dressing or simply boiled and served with drawn butter; chicken laced with savory Smithfield ham as well as an array of other hearty fare. At any meal, room must be saved for both the inn's famous, hot-from-the-oven honey buns and one of the superlative desserts. Whitman's Surprise is a sinful concoction of a heaping mound of coffee ice cream in a pure chocolate shell smothered with a praline sauce.

A small cluster of wonderfully old-fashioned, immaculate rooms are found on the second floor of the

Left: Tall, stately trees shade the outdoor dining deck at the Silvermine. OVERLEAF: A treasure-trove of toys and tools from a bygone era adorn the inn.

Ask the innkeepers about the only woman allowed to stand at a bar in Connecticut.

old tavern and across the street above the inn's country store. Guest rooms might contain a four-poster canopy or ornate Victorian antique bedstead. Boudoir chairs, hooked rugs, and framed prints in each room are just a few of the elements that create a charming atmosphere.

SILVERMINE TAVERN, corner of Perry and Silvermine Aves., Norwalk, CT 06850; (203) 847-4558; Francis Whitman, Sr., and Francis Whitman, Jr., Innkeepers. Rates: *moderate*; continental breakfast included. Open year round, except closed on Tuesdays from September to May; 6 rooms in main building, 4 above country store, all with private baths, some with tub only. Restaurant, open to the public, serves lunch and dinner daily, except Tuesdays from September to May. Children welcome; major credit cards accepted. Silvermine Guild of Artists, with galleries, studios, and workshops, nearby.

DIRECTIONS: From New York City, take Merritt Pkwy. to exit 39; turn onto Rte. 7 south. At first traffic light, turn right on Perry Ave., which winds 2½ miles to tavern.

HOMESTEAD INN

Greenwich   **CONNECTICUT**

A fine inn beautifully restored

Located a scant forty miles from Manhattan in the posh community of Belle Mead, the Homestead Inn is a hybrid; half a cozy country inn filled with charmingly irregular bedchambers, and half a sophisticated watering hole frequented by the cream of Greenwich society. Combining high standards of quality and perfect timing with the right location, innkeepers Nancy Smith and Lessie Davison are attracting knowledgeable inngoers and gourmands alike.

It wasn't always so, however. The Homestead was on its last legs, sagging from neglect, when Lessie and Nancy bought the inn. Reinforcing teetering foundations and ripping away layers of wallpaper, paneling, and suspect "modernizations," the two

Left: The main dining room is a faithfully restored, early colonial barn.

carefully restored this carpenter Gothic treasure, with its broad and inviting veranda and jaunty cupola.

The inn's restaurant is found in an early eighteenth-century barn that was uncovered during the remodeling, to the surprise of everyone. This room is a warm blend of aged barnboards and irregular timbers, salt-glazed crockery and handhooked rugs, a colonial hearth and inset skylights. The attached glass-walled dining porch washes the room with a soft and natural light and offers a grand view of the sweeping lawn with its venerable oaks and maples. Gifted chef Jacques Thiebeult uses the freshest ingredients available from city markets, filling his menu with delightful offerings that include the inn's famous mussel soup billi bi, a pot of snails swimming in pernod-spiked cream, fresh Catskill foie gras, warm chèvre redolent of garlic and herbs, sweetbreads sautéed with wild mushrooms and Madeira, veal kidneys bathed with a Dijon mustard cream, and impeccably fresh Dover sole accented with red caviar.

Lucky are they who dine well and need only tumble into a comfortable bed. In the main inn each guest room door has a second, louvered summer door fitted

The main inn building shows off its wonderful carpentry.

with a lustrous bird's-eye maple doorknob, and all rooms are furnished with an eclectic collection of antiques as well as comfortable prop-up pillows and reading lamps. The Bride's Room with its fishnet canopy and grand proportions is a favorite, as is the Robin Suite, whose sitting room sports original stenciling uncovered during the inn's facelift. Besides the inn proper, two separate houses, a small cottage, and a larger independent house, offer the newest guest accommodations, which range from intimate chambers to commodious and elegant suites.

HOMESTEAD INN, 420 Field Point Rd., Greenwich, CT 06830; (203) 869-7500; Nancy Smith and Lessie Davison, Innkeepers. Rates: *expensive;* continental breakfast included. Open year round; 13 rooms in inn, 3 in cottage, and 8 in independent house, each with private bath, some with showers only; each with telephone and cable TV. Restaurant, open to the public (reservation preferred), serves lunch weekdays and dinner nightly, except Christmas Day, New Year's Day, and Labor Day. Children over 12 welcome; no pets; major credit cards accepted.

DIRECTIONS: From New York City, take I-95 to exit 3 in Greenwich. Turn left off ramp and turn left again onto Horseneck Lane at light just before railroad overpass. At next traffic light, turn left onto Field Point Rd. and continue ¼ mile to inn on your right.

The Sun Porch dining room.
Right: The Sleigh Bed Room.

The Bride's Room.

CAPTAIN STANNARD HOUSE

Westbrook   **CONNECTICUT**

Americana and antiques from top to bottom

After living in Newington, Connecticut, for twenty-seven years, Betty and Al Barnett came to the new England coastal village of Westbrook, where "the town welcomed us with open arms," says Betty.

The object of their affection, upon which they have lavished tender, loving care is The Captain Stannard House. They have restored walls, ceilings, and floors to bring the house back to its original condition.

Acquiring the house in 1977, the Barnetts moved here along with their antiques shop. A country store they set up at the side entrance entices guests with its biscuit tins, tobacco boxes, apothecary jars, an old brass cash register, and two mannequins in seasonal attire. Next to the country store, the antiques shop has samplings of Americana—country pine and maple cupboards, muffin tins, baskets, quilts, stoneware, toys.

Six guest rooms have been restored, and Betty has hand-stenciled each of them. The Captain's Room has strawberry stenciling, two twin four-poster, flame-tipped bedsteads, a Victorian marble-covered chest, and a Hitchcock chair. The American Room, stenciled with red daisies, has an antique brass eagle over the pine cannon-ball bed covered in a Newport eagle bedspread. Lobster carriers are used for luggage racks, and all of the rooms have interesting juts and angles.

Breakfast, included in the rates, consists of juices, a fruit basket, homemade pumpkin, bran, or blueberry muffins, and a cereal parfait frozen and topped with whipped cream and served in a goblet. The Barnetts' daughter makes the popular peach and strawberry jams. Furnished with old tavern tables and ladder-back chairs, the breakfast room is a treasure.

To make absolutely sure there is no end to relaxation the Barnetts have provided an ample, comfortably appointed lounge. Old farm implements cover the walls, and there are two gold tweed sofas, a love seat, a braid rug, trunk and blanket chest coffee tables, card and board games, and two cupboards crammed with books.

Antique jingle bells.

Left: The Breakfast Room displays some of the inn's antiques.

THE CAPTAIN STANNARD HOUSE, 138 South Main Street, Westbrook, CT 06498; (203) 399-7565; Al and Betty Barnett, Innkeepers. Rates: *inexpensive* to *moderate;* expanded continental breakfast included. Open all year; 6 guest rooms, each with private bath, air conditioning, and thermostat. No other meals served. Children over 6 welcome; no pets; Visa, Mastercard, American Express accepted. Close to Mystic Seaport, Essex Village, Goodspeed Opera House, and Valley Railroad steam train.

DIRECTIONS: From I-95 take exit 65 to Westbrook Center and go west 4/10 of a mile on Rte 1. Inn is on left at corner of South Main and Kingfisher Lane.

Old Lyme BEE AND THISTLE INN CONNECTICUT

A sophisticated menu of new American cuisine

Under the thoughtful guidance of new innkeepers Bob and Penny Nelson, the Bee and Thistle Inn has developed a sophisticated menu of new American cuisine and brought popular good dining to Old Lyme, Connecticut. With five chefs in the kitchen (two from the Culinary Institute in New Hyde Park, New York), the emphasis is on fresh ingredients and prepared-to-order food.

Dining here has no pretension to elegance. With comfortable seating in pleasant surroundings, food is the focal point and the selections are interesting and varied. Shrimp Satori, chicken en papillote, roast goose Bordeaux, veal sweetbreads Française, and pesto in a pot are some of the choices. Good wine is offered at affordable prices, so there is no difficulty in complementing a meal. For dessert, a chocolate mousse cake layered with rum-soaked lady fingers and an ice cream peanut pie laden with chocolate chunks and roasted peanuts are hard to resist. On Saturday nights, harp music usually accompanies the candle-light dinners.

Guest rooms have been redone, and there is a mix of comfortable furnishings and simple décor complemented by several canopy beds, oriental and braided carpets, floral wall papers, old chests, and ruffled curtains. On the second and third floors there are wonderful sitting areas in the spacious hallways. Brocaded couches, wing chairs, and potted greenery invite curling up with a good book.

At the turn of the century, the ample aristocratic atmosphere of Old Lyme attracted a whole school of fashionable painters, American Impressionists in love with the varying moods of the landscape and the stately old buildings. Childe Hassam, the most famous of these artists, often painted the soaring Old Lyme Meeting House. In the museum next door to the inn, visitors can see these artists' works, paintings of a light-filled world of pleasure among cultured friends.

To waken in a spacious, sunlit room and be served breakfast in bed, to lunch beneath the spreading trees on the front lawn, to bicycle down the main street to the water, where the Connecticut River meets the sea—these are but a few of the pleasures that await visitors to the inn, who will experience good living at its best.

The Sun Porch is a delightful dining area.

Left: Mornings at the Bee and Thistle begin with breakfast in bed.

BEE AND THISTLE INN, 100 Lyme Street, Old Lyme, CT 06371; (203) 434-1667; Bob and Penny Nelson, Innkeepers. Rates: *moderate.* Open all year; 11 rooms, 9 with private baths, 2 sharing bath. Dining room open to public, serving breakfast, lunch, dinner; guests may have breakfast in bed. Full service bar. Children over 6 welcome; no pets; Visa, MasterCard, American Express accepted. Bicycles for guests at no charge. Historic Essex village, Lyme Art Gallery, Goodspeed Opera House, Valley Railroad steam train nearby.

DIRECTIONS: From I-95 north or south take exit 70 to Old Lyme. Taxi service from Amtrak's Old Saybrook station, which is a stop for New York and Boston trains.

GRISWOLD INN

Essex · CONNECTICUT

Famous for its dining room

Rich in American history, the village of Essex has played an important role in the life of the East Coast since the village's settlement in the 1640s. The first inhabitants chose the location because the banks of the Connecticut River afforded fertile fields and abundant foodstuffs. Within twenty years the river became a primary artery for the distribution of goods from the West Indies, and by the mid-1700s Essex was a thriving center for shipbuilding. The Continental Army's first man-of-war was built in the shipyard of Uriah and John Hayden at the foot of the town's Main Street.

The Griswold Inn has recorded the pulse of the community since the inn's beginnings in 1776. The bar, which was an eighteenth-century schoolhouse complete with horsehair-and-oyster-shell ceiling, is an atmospheric room, whose walls reverberate with a happy babble of voices and which serves as the meeting place and hangout for a wide assortment of colorful locals. The Gris's dining room, built in the 1940s, is among the warmest and handsomest to be found anywhere. Its aged wooden walls and ceiling, taken from an old New England covered bridge, are lined with one of the finest collections of marine art in the country. Currier and Ives steamboat prints, oils by Antonio Jacobsen, and turn-of-the century nautical prints set a mood that is at once masculine and softly romantic. The adjoining Steamboat Room is famed for its painted mural of Essex harbor. With a flick of a switch, the mural undulates, mimicking the movement of a ship on water.

Food at the Griswold is hearty fare, served piping hot and with no pretense. The inn specializes in fresh fish, huge slabs of barbecued baby back ribs, and prime ribs of beef; and the selection of desserts is wide, rich, and totally satisfying. The Sunday Hunt Breakfast is an especially popular happening styled after an English buffet and featuring such dishes as grits and cheddar cheese soufflé, fried chicken, broiled lamb kidneys, and Maine smelts.

Accommodations at the inn are pleasant but housekeeping sometimes leaves something to be desired. A number of suites offer space and extra comforts, though the real and magnetic charm of the Gris is centered in its first-floor common rooms.

The marina is an important part of Essex.

Left: The classic old building is decorated accordingly.
OVERLEAF: The inn's fabled collection of marine art lines the walls of the Tap Room dining room.

GRISWOLD INN, Main St., Essex, CT 06426; (203) 767-0991; William and Victoria Winterer, Innkeepers. Rates: *moderate;* continental breakfast included. Open year round, except Christmas Eve and Christmas Day; 9 rooms in inn, 13 in Annex, all with private baths, some with showers only. Restaurant serves lunch and dinner daily and Sunday "Hunt Breakfast." Children welcome; no pets; all major credit cards accepted. Terrific collection of art and marine memorabilia in public rooms; boating, sailing, sightseeing nearby.

DIRECTIONS: From New York City, take I-95 to Conn. Rte. 9. Take Essex exit 3 onto Rte. 153, which becomes Main St. Inn is in town center.

One of America's great dining experiences

Paul and Louise Ebeltoft brought their own high standards of innkeeping to the already celebrated Copper Beech Inn. Building on the inn's reputation for fine food and dining, they have maintained and even surpassed the spirit of near perfection that abides here.

Three dining rooms are the heart of the inn, and maitre d' Paul Sienkowski hovers over all of them. A lover of fine wines, he also presides over the wine cellar, which features 115 labels ranging from $8 to $650 a bottle.

The Copper Beech Room is the house's original dining room. Covered in a Williamsburg blue-and-white patterned wall covering, it has Empire-style furniture and a blue Chinese rug spread over wide floor boards. The Ivoryton Room has Queen Anne furniture, dusty rose carpeting, and looks out on the inn's wide-spreading copper beech tree—possibly the oldest in Connecticut. Finally the Comstock Room, with its large stone fireplace, has Chippendale chairs, a mahogany Federal table that seats six, a handsome oriental rug, and is named for the ivory merchant who built this house in 1880. Excellent food is carried through these rooms by a skillful and highly trained staff that anticipates every need and leaves the diner feeling like royalty.

Popular entrées include swordfish seasoned with shallots, dill, lemon, and white wine, and a bouillabaisse flavored with saffron, tomato, and pernod. Stuffed roast duckling served with wild lingonberry sauce, Chateaubriand bouquetière, and beef Wellington in a wine and truffle sauce are standard fare. Sacher torte, framboises brûlées (a ramekin of fresh berries marinated in Grand Marnier), and profiterolles—cream puffs filled with ice cream and served with dark chocolate sauce—are well worth disregarding calories.

Five spacious rooms provide wonderful hideaways between meals. The Copper Beech Suite, the inn's largest room, belonged to Mrs. Comstock, wife of the ivory merchant. Country French in feeling, the

Left: A good setting with which to begin a memorable meal.

suite features a king-size French brass bed with floor-to-ceiling canopy, floral wallpaper and couch in tones of blue, a cheerful dining alcove, and a sitting area beside the fireplace. The companion room, originally belonging to Mr. Comstock, is also decorated in shades of blue and has a maple four-poster bed, sculpted-top chest, and soft aqua carpeting. A colonial loveseat near the fireplace and five large windows overlook the well-tended garden.

The Ebeltofts are currently in the process of restoring the original gabled carriage house into nine additional guest rooms. Already distinguished by its cupola, the structure will have skylights, some sleeping lofts, and Jacuzzi baths.

Although the inn was once thought of as very expensive for dining, this is no longer true. The Copper Beech's prices compare favorably with other truly fine restaurants around the country and are reasonable for those who value excellent food and impeccable service.

THE COPPER BEECH INN, Main Street, Ivoryton, CT 06442; (203) 767-0330; Louise and Paul Ebeltoft, Innkeepers. Rates: *moderate;* continental breakfast included. Open all year except Mondays and Christmas Day; 5 rooms with private baths. Celebrated dining rooms open to public, serving lunch and dinner with haute cuisine and unusually attentive service. Children not encouraged; no pets; Visa, MasterCard, American Express, Diners Club accepted. Close to Essex village for marina, shops, and Valley Railroad vintage steam train.

DIRECTIONS: From I-95, north or south, take exit 69 and follow Rte. 9 north to exit 3 and go left 1½ miles to inn. Taxi or limousine service available from Essex marina and Amtrak's Old Saybrook railroad station, which is a stop for Boston and New York trains.

A fine combination of the old and the new, with extras

David and Elise Joslow, the gracious and dynamic innkeepers of The Inn at Chester, have made their former home, the 1776 John B. Parmelee house, into the nucleus of this sprawling country inn. In addition to a handsome barn moved here in the nineteen sixties to function as the family room, the Joslows have recently added two new wings of rooms and public spaces.

Three guest rooms in the original house are colonial in décor, two with fireplaces and one with a sitting room. Tucked under the eaves, small charming bathrooms, with knotty pine walls and ceilings, have delicate porcelain fixtures and vintage etched-glass mirrors.

Comfortably furnished in simple period pieces, rooms in the new wings are more spacious, each one housing a television in its bachelor's chest. Private baths with up-to-the-minute comforts have baskets filled with Gilchrist and Soames' soaps, herb shampoo, bath cubes, and talc.

Meals are served in the old barn, where a dining balcony overlooks all, and high, latticed windows permit a view of the inn's fifteen acres.

Created in a kitchen that is no stranger to four-star chefs, the food is superb. Currently orchestrated by chef Charlie Lamonica, a graduate of the Culinary Institute of America and the famed Breakers in Florida, the new American cuisine is interesting and varied. Mushroom strudel, Cajun shrimp étouffé, pork with plums, cranberry roasted duckling, and tender medallions of venison, in season, are some of an evening's dishes.

With The Inn at Chester, the Joslows have succeeded in attaining the unusual: the perfect blending of an intimately sized inn with the expanded facilities of a small hotel. Besides offering three superb meals, there are extras: room service, a billiard room and library, exercise room with sauna, telecommunications room for workaholics, meeting rooms for groups, stocked bass pond, tennis court, masseuse, and private beach just down the road.

Holiday celebrations are planned for the entire family: the Twelve Days of Christmas festivities include a medieval Christmas dinner featuring partridge, a woodwind trio, and a group of a singing Shakespearean actors. New Year's Eve is celebrated with a gala dinner and dancing to a live orchestra.

Warm wood and low ceilings emanate the cozy feeling of simple life in colonial times.

Left: The lounge at Chester shuts out worldly cares.

THE INN AT CHESTER, 318 West Main Street, Chester, CT 06412; (203) 526-4961; David and Elise Joslow, Innkeepers. Rates: *moderate.* Open all year; 51 rooms with private baths. Dining rooms open to public, serving 3 superb meals and special brunch on Sunday. Children welcome; pets allowed; credit cards accepted. Exercise room, sauna, stocked bass pond, jogging trails, billiards, tennis on premises.

DIRECTIONS: From I-95, north or south, take exit 69. Follow Rte. 9 north to exit 6 and turn west for about 3 miles on Rte. 148 to Chester-Killingworth town line and Inn. Taxi service from Old Saybrook railroad station, where Amtrak's New York and Boston trains stop.

RHODE ISLAND

INN AT CASTLE HILL INNTOWNE

Newport   **RHODE ISLAND**

Sumptuously grand in manner and taste

Like a ship setting out to sea, the Inn at Castle Hill juts into the Atlantic Ocean as boldly as a tall ship in full sail. Renowned naturalist Alexander Agassiz, one of the founders of modern marine biology, built the mansion in 1874 as a summer home, and his choice of location, a narrow peninsula at the mouth of Narragansett Bay, was inspired by his love of the water.

Castle Hill is a weathered-shingle "cottage" with turrets and gables and a sweeping sunporch that overlooks the sea. When innkeeper Paul McEnroe

PREVIOUS PAGE: Evening sunlight casts a golden glow over the inn, which commands the entrance to Newport Harbor. *Left:* A special suite.

took over the management of the inn, he wisely chose to limit the number of bedrooms. Each guest room, therefore, is an original part of Agassiz's home. Luxurious fabrics in a floral motif run throughout, creating a fresh and interesting contrast to the dark depths of the beautiful wood. To supplement the number of overnight accommodations, the inn offers simpler rooms in the separate Harbour House, a low-slung, shingled structure, and in a string of plain but comfortable beach cottages that are taken for a week or longer. In order to satisfy the need for more rooms, Paul and his wife, Betty, converted a commercial building in the heart of Newport into a posh and intimate inn called simply Inntowne. It is decorated in the same fresh florals as her waterside counterpart, but here, guests enjoy afternoon tea in the antiques-filled breakfast room as well as beach privileges at Castle Hill.

Besides the grandeur of its setting and appearance, Castle Hill is well known for its fine kitchen. As fits the mood, the evening meal is a formal affair, with jackets required. Chef James Mitchell excels at deli-

Room 9. Thorton Wilder describes the view from this room in his book *Theophilus North*.

The finest food. The finest service. The finest china. *Right*, the Inntowne's breakfast room.

cate and savory sauces and draws raves for such dishes as snails sautéed with cepes, brandy, and cream, served in a light pastry; a hot fish terrine in a shimmering pool of crayfish sauce; veal sweetbreads accompanied by Westphalian ham and dressed in a capered lemon butter; and a delicately breaded boneless breast of chicken stuffed with banana and napped with a tangy raspberry sauce.

THE INN AT CASTLE HILL, Ocean Dr., Newport, RI 02840; (401) 849-3800; Paul McEnroe, Innkeeper. Rates: *moderate* to *expensive*, depending on season; continental breakfast included. Open year round; 12 rooms in inn, 6 in Harbour House, 18 in beach cottages, with private and shared baths. Dining room, open to the public by reservation, serves daily from Easter to November, and 4 days a week in the off-season (November, December, April, May); closed January to Easter. Not recommended for children, no pets; Visa, MasterCard accepted. Three private beaches; golf and tennis nearby.

DIRECTIONS: From downtown Newport, take Bellevue Ave., which becomes Ten Mile Ocean Dr. Follow it, watching for inn sign on left. Or take Thames St. to Ocean Dr. and turn right; watch for inn sign on right just beyond Coast Guard station. *Note:* For information on the bed & breakfast, Inntowne, call Betty McEnroe or manager Eileen Reed at (401) 846-9200.

Each guest room is dramatically different.

THE 1661 INN
HOTEL MANISSES

Block Island

RHODE ISLAND

A charming addition on Block Island

After a lifelong romance with Block Island, Justin and Joan Abrams bought island property, which included a small white hotel. Renaming it The 1661 Inn—after the year Block Island was settled—the Abrams became part of the island's history, dating back to the Manissean Indians. More recently the Abrams have added Hotel Manisses, a carefully restored Victorian building, to their holdings.

At The 1661 Inn, oceanfront rooms, all furnished in colonial manner, have private decks with a marvelous and soothing view. The small strip of land, tucked between the inn and the vast blue Atlantic, harbors two small duck ponds, a fragrant meadow, and pretty flower gardens, providing a memorable tableau while enjoying the daily Wine and Nibble hour on the upper deck.

Included in the rates is a fisherman's breakfast, the only meal served at the inn. Scrambled eggs, assorted muffins, fresh fruit, corned beef hash, baked beans, and a daily special, like seafood Newburg or pasta primavera, is served buffet-style in the floral-papered dining room overlooking the ocean.

Distinguished by its Victorian furnishings, Hotel Manisses has carved, marble-top chests; deep-well Victorian bureaus; delicate lace curtains; rich velvet bedspreads; and ornately carved brass bedsteads. Sixteen rooms have private baths and four Jacuzzis. Its restaurant specializes in the island's catch—Block Island swordfish, striped bass, and bluefish—and serves orange or raspberry duck and beef dishes. It is a popular eating spot for the entire island. The Abrams' garden furnishes fresh vegetables, and when a storm grounded the island's ferries for days, Hotel Manisses was the only establishment serving fresh vegetables.

A happy hour in the restaurant features hot hors d'oeuvres such as chicken livers and bacon, fried clams, and an assortment of canapés. A fully stocked bar features popular local concoctions like one island favorite prepared with rum, Midori, and pineapple juice. Upstairs in the lobby, high tea is staged daily. Ham salad, chicken salad, and other tea sandwiches and finger pastries are served with coffee and tea.

With the assistance of daughter, Rita, and son-in-law Steve, the Abrams have built a thriving family business. The Manisses Attic, an antiques shop they opened on the main street, features treasures gathered during the hotel's restoration.

THE 1661 INN, Box I, Block Island, RI 02807; (401) 466-2421; Joan and Justin Abrams, Rita and Steve Draper, Innkeepers. Rates: *moderate* with shared baths, *expensive* with private baths, both including full breakfast. Open mid-May to mid-Oct., annex open all year; 15 guest rooms at inn, 10 in annex, private and shared baths. Guests take dinner at Hotel Manisses (see below). Children over 6 welcome; no pets; Visa, MasterCard, American Express accepted. Car rentals, ocean swimming, boating nearby.

HOTEL MANISSES. Rates: *inexpensive* to *moderate;* full breakfast included. Contact as above. Open April 1 to Nov. 1; 17-room restored Victorian hotel with private baths and Jacuzzis. Dining room serves lunch and dinner. Children over 10 only; no pets; credit cards and directions as above.

DIRECTIONS: Take I-95 to New London, Conn. for island ferry (car reservations a must). In summer ferries also run from Pt. Judith, Providence, and Newport, R.I. In winter, from Pt. Judith only. For schedules write Interstate Navigation, Box 482, New London, CT 06320.

A guest room at the Hotel Manisses, with its own Jacuzzi.

Left: The inn stands on a rise overlooking Block Island and the sea.

OVERLEAF: *Above,* the Hotel Manisses, beautifully restored; *below,* the hotel's parlor.